WHY AREN'T ECONOMISTS AS IMPORTANT AS GARBAGEMEN?

WHY AREN'T ECONOMISTS AS IMPORTANT AS GARBAGEMEN?

Essays on the State of Economics

DAVID COLANDER

M. E. SHARPE, INC.
ARMONK, NEW YORK
LONDON, ENGLAND

Copyright © 1991 by M. E. Sharpe, Inc.

Available in the United Kingdom and Europe from M. E. Sharpe, Publishers, 3 Henrietta Street, London WC2E 8LU.

Library of Congress Cataloging-in-Publication Data

Colander, David C.
Why aren't economists as important as garbagemen? : and other essays on the state of economics / by David C. Colander.
p. cm.
Includes bibliographical references (p.   ) and index.
ISBN 0-87332-776-4 (cloth). — ISBN 0-87332-777-2 (paper)
1. Economics—Methodology. 2. Economists. I. Title.
HB131.C65   1991
330'.092'2—dc20   90-8841
                                                                         CIP

Printed in the United States of America.

∞

BB   10   9   8   7   6   5   4   3   2   1

This book is dedicated to
Robert L. Basmann
Bob Clower
Lauchlin Currie
Nicholas Georgescu-Roegen
and
Gordon Tullock
who, each in his own way, have worked to make economists
more important than garbagemen.

Contents

Part 4: Critics of Economics

Acknowledgments

The essays in this book did not spring up as a phoenix from the fire. They developed in complementary conversations with a group of economists who share my vision of what economics ought to be and in not-so-complementary conversations with a group of economists who don't share my vision.

Some of the economists who deserve specific thanks for their role in shaping my views or in commenting on the essays include: Bradley Bateman, Samuel Bostoph, Reuven Brenner, Bruce Caldwell, Robert Clower, Bob (A.W.) Coats, Richard Cornwall, James Galbraith, Craufurd Goodwin, Robert Heilbroner, Charles Kindleberger, Arjo Klamer, Kenneth Koford, Harry Landreth, Axel Leijonhufvud, Donald McCloskey, Phillip Mirowski, Dimitri Papadimitriou, Yngve Ramstad, Cordelia Reimers, Warren Samuels, Amartya Sen, Robert Solow, Paul Streeten, Gordon Tullock, Hal Varian, Paul Wendt, Nancy Wulwick, and Leland Yeager. I leave for the reader to decide who belongs in which of the two groups.

Besides these economists, there are also my students who have read these essays at various stages, my research assistant, Ayez Haque, my family, and my personal editor, Helen Reiff (who has also processed the copy to disks for the publisher and done the index). I thank them all. Thanks also go to Richard Bartel, Aud Thiessen, and Alexandra Koppen of M.E. Sharpe, Inc. and the copy editor, Ann Grogg. All did superb jobs.

Some of these essays have been previously published, and I

would like to thank the publishers for giving me permission to reprint them here.

The title essay, "Why Aren't Economists as Important as Garbagemen?" originally appeared in the July 1987 issue of the *Journal of Economic and Monetary Affairs*. The Geonomics Institute in Middlebury, Vermont, which sponsored its original publication, has given me permission to use the essay.

"The Making of an Economist," written jointly with Arjo Klamer, is reprinted by permission of Arjo Klamer and the *Journal of Economic Perspectives*. This material first appeared in the Fall 1987 issue.

"Workmanship, Incentives, and Cynicism" initially appeared in *The Making of an Economist* by Arjo Klamer and David Colander, copyright Westview Press, Boulder, Colorado, 1990, and is reprinted with permission.

"The Invisible Hand of Truth" originally appeared in *The Spread of Economic Ideas*, edited by David Colander and A.W. Coats, copyright Cambridge University Press, New York, 1989. Cambridge University Press has given me permission to reprint it here.

"The Evolution of Keynesian Economics: From Keynesian to New Classical to New Keynesian" was originally published in *Keynes and Public Policy after Fifty Years*, edited by Omar F. Hamouda and John N. Smithin and published by Edward Elgar and New York University Press, Aldershot, England, 1989, and is reprinted here with their permission.

"Galbraith and the Theory of Price Control" originally appeared in the *Journal of Post Keynesian Economics*, Fall 1984, and is reprinted with permission from M.E. Sharpe, Inc.

"Form and Content in Appraising Recent Economic Developments" will be published in the June 1991 issue of *Methodus* and is reprinted here with permission of the International Network for Economic Method.

WHY AREN'T ECONOMISTS AS IMPORTANT AS GARBAGEMEN?

Introduction

Some of my best friends are economists; I say this at the beginning of this collection of essays because, while the title suggests that I, like Brutus, have come to bury economists and economics, I have actually come to praise them. Oh, I criticize all right, but that criticism is based upon a belief that economics is important and that it has an important contribution to make to the public policy debate. I wouldn't waste my time criticizing economics and the economics profession unless I believed them important.

The Positive and Negative Themes

The essays have two themes: a positive one and a negative one. The positive theme of the essays is that economic analysis, if kept in perspective, is enormously powerful. It provides a way of uncovering the workings of real-world phenomena that fit the perceptions many people have. The negative theme is that economic analysis is not being kept in perspective by economists, and that loss of perspective means that much of what comes out under the name of economic research has little or no value for society. But even this negative theme has positive overtones in demonstrating the power of economic analysis.

What is happening in the economics profession becomes much more understandable when one looks at it from an economist's standpoint. Economists have often turned the laser edge of their analysis on the legal profession, the medical profession, and the world in general but, to my knowledge, no economist has turned economic analysis upon itself and considered the economics of the economics profession. Somehow economists have been all too willing to accept that other people are greedy, self-interested maximizers, but none of them have had the audacity to look at themselves as that same breed—no better, no worse, than the rest of the world. I've never been accused of lacking audacity.

Looking at the profession using an economic perspective requires audacity because, when one uses economic analysis to study the economics profession, what one sees is not very pretty. What one sees is the following: Academic economists, following their own self-interest, have diverted economic analysis from looking at real issues to playing mind-games that are fun for academic economists but of little use for society. Academic economists are allowed to continue these mind-games because what they do is not subject to the test of the market. What's happened in the economics profession is a wonderful example of what economic reasoning says will happen to any group in society that is not subject to market forces.

The Power of Economic Reasoning

Throughout the essays in this book I attack the economics profession, but I do so because I have enormous respect for the power of economic reasoning. There's far too little of it in the world. What do I mean by economic reasoning? I mean neo-classical economic reasoning: analyzing the economy using the assumption that individuals are relatively self-interested and figuring out the strategic decisions these self-interested individuals are likely to make given the institutions that exist, while keeping the economists' personal feelings about what is good and bad out of the analysis, as best one can. I strongly believe that economic reasoning provides one with a powerful tool of analysis. It allows one to portray complicated systems in a relatively simple way and to cut through years of specific institutional study. Economic reasoning cuts to the quick.

Throughout the debates I see currently under way about day care, rights for the disabled, welfare, support for the arts, I ask myself: Why hasn't economic reasoning influenced the debate? Why doesn't economic reasoning play a larger role?

The reason is that most academic economists aren't subjecting such issues to economic reasoning. Instead they are using economic reasoning to analyze issues that no one besides economists are interested in, either because their discussion of the issues is so abstract that it cannot be applied to economic reality or because they have made such far out assumptions that the applicability of the analysis is, at best, tangential. Economists have retreated into the domain of abstract theory. By applying their analysis to issues no one except economists cares about, economists avoid upsetting people.

It's other communicators, such as Charles Murray or Robert Samuelson, neither of whom is formally trained as an economist, who are applying economic analysis to real-world events with reasonable objectivity. They upset people, but that's precisely what good economic analysis does. It forces people to look at reality from a different perspective than most people use—a perspective that magnifies the individualist motives of individuals and attempts to maintain a nonpartisan view of social reality, even when being nonpartisan requires one to challenge existing social conventions. To see what I mean, let's consider an example.

In one of his *Newsweek* columns, Robert Samuelson (1988) challenged government funding for the arts, claiming that it was an elitist grab for money by a favored few. He argued that rodeos are as deserving, or more deserving, of funding. From an individualistic standpoint, he was, of course, right, but that standpoint differed significantly from that of most readers of the column, and he was strongly criticized by most readers. But I suspect he got a few of them to think about the issue.

It isn't quite true that no economists are applying economic reasoning to real-world events. Conservative economists, such as Milton Friedman, George Stigler, and the George Mason "mafia" have consistently applied economic analysis to just about every imaginable issue. But they do more than apply economic analysis; they also believe it—they see individualism as morally correct and they support "free market" policies as a moral position, not a reasoned position. For those who agree that individualism is the fundamental tenet of morality, the conservative economists' approach is convincing, but for those who take a different view of individualism, as the majority of academic society does, the work of these conservative economists is simply an expression of their morality, hardly the stuff objective analysis is made of. Their analysis is discarded as ideological fluff. That leaves it to liberal economists to apply economic reasoning objectively to real-world problems.

But, with few exceptions, liberal economists are extremely hesitant to apply economic analysis to real-world situations because it often comes to results that don't fit their moral view of how things should be. Since they don't have a totally individualistic morality, the conclusions of economic analysis don't match their views of policy. Their response to this problem is to retreat into abstract theory so they don't have to confront the contradiction that what they morally believe is not what their analysis comes to. That, in my view, is the wrong response.

Liberals would be in a much stronger position if they simply admitted that economic reasoning is not the be-all and end-all. Its usefulness is as a rough-and-ready tool to study things one doesn't know much about and doesn't have time to find out. After one has done an economic analysis of an issue, one still must decide whether economic reasoning comes to a reasonable conclusion. To do so, one must integrate social morality into the analysis and have detailed knowledge of the institutions. Only after doing that can economics be appropriately applied to real-world issues. Were liberals to do that, they could play a positive role in real-world economic debates.

An Overview of the Essays

The essays in this volume were written over the last five years. Many were invited essays for economics conferences. As my, I hope, good-natured criticism of the economics profession has become better known over the last few years, I have received many invitations to present my views at conferences and lectures. As I have done so, I have tried to fill in the various aspects of my views, each time presenting an essay on a different aspect of the issues. In doing so I have straightened out my thinking about what my criticisms are. This collection of essays is the finished result, and I believe it provides a good survey of my views.

Part 1 considers economics and policy—what is normally called welfare economics. The title essay, "Why Aren't Economists as Important as Garbagemen?" looks at economists as self-interested maximizers. The essay is written with humor, but its message is deadly serious and in my view provides a succinct statement about what is wrong with economics. Economics tries to do too much—to be too objective, to be too fair. The only way economics can do that is to make itself irrelevant, and that's what it has done.

That essay is a broadside attack on welfare economics and the use of the Pareto-optimal criterion that most economists use. That Pareto-optimal criterion is a simple one: A policy an economist recommends should make everyone better off and no one worse off. In the essay I argue that Pareto optimality is not a criterion economists should use in making policy recommendations. Instead, economists should use an alternative criterion which might be called the *reasonable person criterion*: A policy an economist recommends should be one a reasonable person, when presented with the best information about the costs and benefits of the policy that can be provided, would accept if that person were an outside observer. Some economists, like Tibor Scitovsky, have tried to arrive at the reasonable person criterion from the Pareto-optimal criterion, but the path is too indirect and confuses the issue. The reasonable person criterion isn't derivative of the Pareto criterion; the Pareto criterion is derivative of the reasonable person criterion.

The second essay, "The Best as the Enemy of the Good," extends the analysis in the Garbageman essay and emphasizes the point. Until economists give up the Pareto criterion and replace it with the reasonable person criterion, economics is doomed to irrelevancy. The point I make in that essay is that workaday economists have given up the Pareto criterion; they have become part of the process and are doing what good economists should be doing. They are applying economic reasoning to real-world events and making economics relevant. Academic economists should learn from them, not the other way around.

Part 2 considers the economics profession directly and explains why economists do what they do. Two of the essays in Part 2 are relatively well known to economists. "The Making of an Economist," written jointly with Arjo Klamer, was a highly popular article that helped force the economics establishment to reconsider what it was doing in graduate schools. The approach we followed was simple: We surveyed graduate students at elite schools. Surveying was a novel technique for economists to use, and so not only was our subject matter unusual, so was our technique.

The article was so popular that we extended our consideration of the profession into a book, which we also entitled *The Making of an Economist*. This book included interviews with graduate students that reinforced the arguments made in the article.

In the article, we carefully kept our views out of the analysis; we refused to draw conclusions because we believed that we wouldn't have the space to explain our views and that the survey results spoke for themselves. In the book, we were no longer careful; after the interviews, we each wrote our own interpretation of the survey and interview results. The essay "Workmanship, Incentives, and Cynicism" is my interpretation of the survey and interviews and hence of the state of economics.

In that essay one sees both themes of this volume expressed. The negative theme is reflected in my characterization of what currently goes on in economics as self-serving game playing. But that characterization comes from applying economic analysis to scientific methodology.

An Economic Approach to the Philosophy of Science

Most approaches to scientific methodology assume that scientists are searching for the truth. No theory of the philosophy of science has developed which does not assume that. Economic analysis forces one to ask the question: Is that—the assumption that scientists search for the truth—an appropriate assumption? That's the strength of economic reasoning; it forces one to ask difficult questions.

Using an economic theory of methodology, one must give up the assumption of truth-seeking scientists. People do not search for the truth; they maximize utility. If institutions guide their actions so that maximizing utility and searching for the truth overlap, then a science is progressive; otherwise it is regressive.

This economic theory of the philosophy of science is enormously strong; it extends beyond the sociological and rhetorical approaches to methodology, which simply look at what happens in science, and provides a theory of why what happens in science happens. In doing so, it brings out the importance of institutions in judging what happens in the world. It also shows a fundamental flaw in Friedman's positive theory of neo-classical economic methodology. Friedman argues that the goal of the economist should be predictive and that economists adopt the theory with the most predictive power. But self-interested people will adopt only those theories that maximize their utility, and it is not at all clear why theories with the most predictive power maximize economists' utility.

In the next essay, "The Invisible Hand of Truth," I extend the "Workmanship" essay and argue that the theories economists choose do not reflect a search for the truth. They reflect short-term interests, and that's why economics has lost its bearings.

I should make clear that my description of "what is" is not a description of "what should be." I believe scientists should search for the truth and that institutions should be designed to lead scientists to do so. But assuming scientists search for the truth doesn't make scientists search for the truth. Institutions and incentives make scientists search for the truth, and any progressive science or discipline must pay close attention to the incentives that guide scientists' actions.

An Economic Approach to the Author

All the above articles are about the economics profession. The profession has been the primary focus of my research for the last five years. That was not always my focus, however. I went into economics to study economics, not the economics profession. Looking at the economics profession represented a switch in research focus for me—away from research on economic issues and toward an analysis of the profession. The two essays in Part 3 bridge the gap between that abstract research I was doing and my research on the profession. They explain why I switched.

To understand them one needs a sense of my earlier research. That research concerned thinking about economic systems in very abstract terms; it concerned thinking about how to integrate microeconomics and macroeconomics, how to formulate the theoretical underpinnings of macroeconomic policy, how to model aggregate disequilibrium market economies, and how market economies could be improved.

I was not a successful researcher. There was a problem with all my research—a serious problem—that led to one rejection after another of my articles. I took the rejections seriously, but not personally, and tried to understand what was wrong with my arguments. What was I not understanding? Where was my logic flawed? I never did find out, because my articles were not rejected for flawed logic. They were rejected for another reason, one that prevented serious discussion or consideration of those ideas.

The problem was not necessarily in my arguments, which I

believe were right but which may be wrong; the problem was in my presentation of the arguments. The reviewers never got to my arguments because the way in which I presented them was wrong. I had no formal model; the framework of analysis was outside what journal editors and reviewers found acceptable.

This introduction is not the place to discuss how much flexibility in form researchers should have in presenting arguments. That's a complicated question, and I've come to realize that what happened to my articles is understandable, although lamentable. Just about every profession establishes a formal method of presenting ideas.

What is not understandable to me, and what led me to start looking at the economics profession rather than economics, was that I couldn't even get most economists to understand my arguments informally. Somehow thinking informally about very abstract issues was not something that most economists could do. Their minds seemed compartmentalized. They thought about economic theory in a highly formal way, but when they thought about economic policy, they often left their abstract analysis aside and relied on pedestrian analysis. They'd talk about policy, but not in an imaginative or creative way. It was that inability to discuss complicated economic issues in an informal way with my fellow economists which led me to change my focus from abstract research to the economics profession itself. If I couldn't discuss complicated ideas informally with most other academic economists, I decided there is something wrong with most other academic economists, not something wrong with me. Reflecting on what has happened in the profession over the last fifty years has led me to believe that many academic economists have become so enamored with formal modeling that they have lost the ability to think outside of formal modeling. When that happens, the models can become ends in themselves rather than tools of analysis.

Part 3 provides some evidence consistent with that view. The first essay, ''The Evolution of Keynesian Economics,'' discusses the broad evolution of macroeconomic thinking from the 1940s to today and argues that the evolution neatly fits the economic theory of the philosophy of science. Economic researchers choose models that maximize their utility, not those that necessarily shed light on the truth. In discussing that theory I differentiate the internal needs of researchers (to publish and to teach) from their external needs (to find a model that best sheds light on reality).

I make no claims that the essay "proves" that theory, nor is it meant to do so. The last thing I'd want to do is to generate a growth industry in analyzing how much internal criteria and how much external criteria drive economic theories. The essay simply presents an idea of how to look at the evolution of economic theories. It's an idea to keep in the back of one's mind. It's not an alternative theory; it's a complementary theory. It's a theory that should be considered by economists but, in my view, should not be pursued in detail by economists because what happens in any particular area of science will be institutionally specific. It's a question to be left for philosophers of science. Considering a theory but not trying formally to prove or disprove it is something that should be done more often than it is. When dealing with abstract issues that are not subject to acceptable formal empirical tests, one must keep a whole group of theories in the back of one's mind.

The second essay in Part 3, "Economic Methodology, Macroeconomics, and Externalities," was the keynote address at the 1988 Pennsylvania Economic Association meetings. It is the most technical of the essays in the collection, and because it deals with specific models in economics it requires a relatively firm background in economics to understand. Nonetheless, the gist of the argument should be apparent to all readers: The disequilibrium adjustment story that economists tell to accompany the aggregate supply/aggregate demand model which forms the basis of the mainstream approach to macroeconomics taught in undergraduate economics doesn't fit reality. Since that story is a necessary part of the model, the model itself is logically flawed. In short, what economists are teaching in introductory economics is wrong. The aggregate supply/aggregate demand model provides nice questions to ask on exams, but it provides little or no help in understanding the economy. Most economists agree with me, but most do not care. I don't know of a much better example of the sorry state into which the academic economics profession has fallen.

The essay ends with a brief presentation of my alternative interpretation of aggregate supply/aggregate demand analysis, which, I argue, fits reality much better. The argument in this essay ties together my initial work in macroeconomics and my economic theory of the philosophy of science. It also provides an economic analysis of why I'm doing what I'm doing. My formal research was going nowhere, so to maximize my utility, and to keep my job, I switched to writing more popular articles, at which I had a comparative advantage. My criticism of the economics profession is a reflection of my inability to succeed at economics as it is currently practiced.

I don't know whether the above economic analysis of my motives is true or not. I'd like to think that I am searching for the truth and that it was commitment to the truth, not my self-interest, which guided my research interest. I don't know what would have happened had I been better at formal economics. Nor does it matter. You, the reader, must judge my arguments. They might be true even if they do reflect my self-interest, and they might be false even if they express my selfless search for the truth.

Critics of Economics

Given my proclivities, it would seem natural that I would gravitate toward the critics of the profession, which I have. The essays in Part 4 are my reflections on the critics of economics. The first essay, "Galbraith and the Theory of Price Control," discusses John Kenneth Galbraith, one of the twentieth-century's most important critics of economics. Any serious economist can have only the highest regard for Galbraith's mind, writing ability, and creativity—whether one agrees with his arguments or not. What is amazing to me, however, is not how successful he's been but how unsuccessful he's been in influencing the economics profession. His work has little influenced the profession. Given his abilities, he should have had a much stronger influence on economics. In the essay I explore a little-known book by Galbraith, the one that led him to forsake economics and economists and turn to writing for the broader public. He's been extraordinarily successful, but his success, I argue, came at a high cost to the economics profession.

Galbraith is among the best of the critics, and his chosen path gives one of the reasons why economics has followed the path it has. Given how easy it is for critics of economics to do well outside the profession, there's little incentive for them to stay in.

The second essay, "Tearing Down Economists' Worlds," deals with critics more generally. It suggests that there is a serious question whether critics want to tear down mainstream economics. We critics are no better, or worse, than mainstream economists. We maximize utility. The search for understanding may be an argument in critics' utility function, but then again it may not be.

I argue that if the role of the critic is to present his or her view in a way that is most likely to make it the mainstream view, then critics are not going about it in the most propitious manner. They discuss ideas with little thought as to how ideas are propagated and how they can foster work in their ideas. I argue that an economic world can only be replaced by another economic world, which means not only must the critics' ideas be better, but also that the expected utility of following those ideas for students must be higher. Critics must provide publication outlets, doable dissertation topics for bright but not brilliant researchers, and job possibilities. These considerations, as much as the understanding ideas convey, govern what ideas will be accepted by students.

I follow the same line of reasoning in the next essay, "Form and Content in Appraising Recent Economic Developments," only this time the group of critics I consider are historians of economic thought, a subgroup of economists who are generally critical of the current state of economics. In the essay I argue that historians of thought have failed the profession for the opposite reason that the economics profession has failed society. Historians of thought have dealt primarily with ideas and have not taught young historians of thought techniques that could have allowed them to move ahead in the economics profession. I argue that the content of ideas is not enough. The form is also important, and a consideration of form should be a serious part of any economist's education. My complaint against the teaching of mainstream economics is that it focuses almost entirely on form; my complaint against the teaching of the history of economic thought is that it focuses almost entirely on content and, in doing so, it doesn't provide the skills students need to succeed in the economics profession.

The final essay of the book, "In Defense of Mainstream Economics," reflects on mainstream economics and the critics and provides a summary judgment of where I stand on the economics profession and what its likely future is. I conclude that for all its failings, mainstream economics still has much to be said for it and will remain in control of the profession for years to come.

The Essays in Perspective

After reading the essays, my students asked me whether it was my intention to alienate all possible groups of economists. That may have been a subconscious motive, but it certainly was not a conscious motive. The conscious motive was simply to consider, as clearly as I could, how I saw the economics profession working and ideas being selected as mainstream. That consideration led me to the belief that the invisible hand of truth is not working too well at guiding the direction of economics, and if that's the case it may not be guiding other disciplines very well. But contrary to what some of my critics have suggested, my consideration of the profession is not a statement of cynical defeatism. It is the exact opposite. If a discipline changes, it is because of informed complaints about what the discipline is doing and because of what critics of the discipline are doing. I see my challenges as part of the process through which the invisible hand of truth operates. If those challenges are viewed as correct by some members of the profession, the pressure for changes will increase. And who knows? Maybe some day economists will be more important than garbagemen.

1

Economists
and Policy

1

Why Aren't Economists as Important as Garbagemen?

Say that all garbagemen got together and went on strike. What would the effect on society be? The answer is clear: Society would be a mess. Now say that all economists got together and went on strike. What would the effect on society be? Most people's answer would be, "None. Things would be just about the same with or without economists." Hence the question: Why aren't economists as important as garbagemen?

That rhetorical question sets up an unfair comparison. To contrast the two roles adequately, one would need to qualify the comparison in innumerable ways, but it does highlight economists' lack of a direct role in the everyday functioning of the economy. Economists simply don't play much of a direct role. When they do play a role, that role is often a cameo—their advice is used if it supports what the proponents want and totally ignored if it does not. An entire movement in economic policy, such as supply-side economics, can develop, influence policy, and fade away with little or no input from economists. Put simply, economists are not directly involved in the functioning of the economy.

In this lack of direct involvement, economics differs from many other professions. For example, in the above comparison, were one to replace economists with doctors, lawyers, or engineers, one's answer would be different; although these groups are still not as directly important as garbagemen, they play a more integral role than do economists in the everyday functioning of society.[1]

Economists' role could be different; there are numerous more active roles economists could play. For example, they might follow the lawyer pattern and play a "certification" role: Any law Congress passed that affected the economy and any decision business executives made that significantly affected the economy, such as plant closings or price changes, might require certification as "economically healthful" by a council of economic advisors. Thus, before a tax cut could be instituted or a major public works program begun, the proposals would need to be ruled upon by an independent economic judiciary.

A less directly involved role might be modeled on doctors' or engineers' roles. If a doctor says you need an operation, you might get a second opinion, but if the two doctors concur, you are likely to have the operation. To some degree, this currently happens with economists but, more often than not, economists' specialized knowledge is used to support already decided-upon positions, is ignored, or is used in a "cover your backside" role.[2] Somehow, policy makers simply do not believe that economists' specialized knowledge is a necessary input into the decision-making process.

It is not surprising that economists are not perceived in the same light as doctors or lawyers. Whereas a majority of doctors and lawyers practice medicine and law, the majority of Ph.D. economists teach; few economists "practice" economics. This means that when doctors and lawyers teach, they are teaching how to "do" medicine and law; when economists teach, because they are not "doing" economics, what they teach is not necessarily determined by what economists do.

At many community colleges and less prestigious four-year colleges, where faculty are given course loads of four or five courses per semester, economists have no time for anything but teaching. At the more prestigious four-year colleges and at universities, that teaching function is complemented by a research function that takes as much, or more, of the economists' time as does their teaching. A "normal teaching load" is two to three classes meeting a total of three hours per week for two fifteen-week semesters. That is a total of 225 hours per year or about 4.5 hours per week with four weeks off for vacation. At research universities, teaching loads are about half that. Academic bureaucracy, course preparation, grading, and following the literature take varying amounts of time, but assuming economists devote twenty hours a week to these activities during the school year at the higher-level schools, economists can devote half their time to research. Economists' role in the functioning of society comes from this research.

When economists talk to other economists about their work, it is this research that they are talking about. Graduate schools are designed primarily to prepare economists to conduct this research, and economists' indirect influence on the policies and activities of government and business stems in large part from this research. Considering the nature of this research clarifies why economists' role is indirect. Their research is basic, rather than applied, and even the applied research is generally presented in a form that is unintelligible to noneconomists; little or no interpretation is provided. Its effect on policy, if it has an effect, occurs through interpreters.

Focusing on basic research is not necessarily bad; nor does engaging in these pursuits mean that economists' role is smaller than other professionals'. It does, however, make their role indirect. Keynes may well be right; economists' long-run indirect role may be of major importance for the economy: Monetary policy, fiscal policy, and the market itself are tombstones to earlier economists' scribblings. Economists' research has also provided an empirical basis that will underlie future policy changes and that limits others in their excessive claims for new policies. For example, although economists did not play a direct role in the supply-side revolution, their empirical work provided a counterweight to supply-side enthusiasm. Thus, economist-bashing is not in order.

Despite their successes, there is a lingering concern about the relevance of much of that research. When teaching others about a subject becomes the main activity of a profession, the subject matter can become more and more removed from what the profession is teaching about. The subject can become self-contained; it can lose its focus, and the research can become elaborate mind-games designed to give students hoops to jump through and economists activities to keep them occupied, rather than contributing to our economic understanding. There are indications that this has happened in economics. The questions economists debate seem to many to be the modern-day equivalent of such scholastic questions as "God is omnipotent; can He create a rock so heavy He cannot lift it?" While debating these "important" questions, economists leave the "unimportant" questions of policy implementation to lawyers, politicians, and special interest groups.

Economists' role has not always been indirect. When economics began, teaching and abstract research were sidelines; economists wrote for policy makers rather than for economists. Classical economists used contextual heuristic arguments that required a reader to bring to the reading of their work a sensitivity to institutions, politics, and moral considerations. They would make arguments that "made sense" to a normal lay reader and were designed to convince that reader.

As economics evolved in the nineteenth and twentieth centuries it moved away from the contextual argumentation that required the reader and writer to share a sense of the institutional framework and into noncontextual argumentation in which the assumptions and institutional framework of their argument were precisely spelled out. Economists came to wear two hats and used contextual or noncontextual arguments, depending on the audience. By the late 1960s, the formal techniques necessary to undertake the noncontextual arguments had become so great that younger economists were no longer being trained to know about real-world institutions, a requirement if one is going to talk seriously about policy.[3]

Unless an economist has inherent or independently acquired

abilities in communicating ideas to the outside world, becoming an economist is like joining a priesthood sworn to communicate only among its members. For economists, if one's arguments can be understood by outsiders they are obviously too simple; if one's work has direct policy relevance, one must be doing something wrong.[4] With such beliefs, it is little wonder that economists are less important to the everyday functioning of the economy than are garbagemen.

Many economists, citing the reasons given above, argue that this separation between economists and the public is necessary. They argue that physicists and mathematicians are not required to communicate with the general public; why should economists? I agree with this argument for a small few in the profession, but there are many more economists than theoretical physicists, and most are not working on the borders of our understanding. Thus, in the case of the majority of economists, I disagree; their role should be similar to that of doctors or engineers. For them, applying and communicating their research to the general public should be an important consideration.

Economists' Perception of Their Role in Society

Economists do not play a more direct role because they have a fundamentally incorrect view of the nature of their role. Economists are trained to be detached in their analysis of the economy—to view themselves as outside the economy—looking down from above. From that perspective, they make judgments on how well the economy is functioning. This is in direct contrast to individuals who view society from their own perspective: When faced with a problem, most people ask, "How will it affect me?" Economists ask, "How will it affect society?" Economists see themselves as outside judges.

Placing any group in an outside position "judging society" is a dangerous undertaking. One is left with the problem: Who will judge the judges? Economists have taken this concern to heart and have worked hard at eliminating their own individualistic perspective and replacing it with "society's perspective." Economists have not been totally successful in eliminating values from their analysis, but they have been partially successful.

However, economists' Don Quixote-like quest for the ideological purity of value-free perspective has come at a cost. In trying to achieve the impossible—avoiding all value judgments in their analysis—they have eliminated their direct role in policy.

In order to stay out of the fray, economists have retreated into pure theory and basic research, leaving to others the "unimportant" role of interpreting the "pure theory" and applying their ideas to society. It is as if a judge, for fear of bringing his own, rather than the law's, perspective to a case, will decide only hypothetical cases.

Taking an outside perspective and attempting to remain value-free is wrong, but not, as some economists have suggested, because it is impossible. The fact that it is impossible to be totally value-free does not mean that economists should not attempt to be as value-free as possible. It is wrong because it is too heavy a burden for any group to bear. Economists are not the judges of the economy; society is. Economists are inside society; their existence as a group reflects society's investment in protecting, modifying, and changing economic institutions.

Viewing economists from an inside perspective changes the nature of their role. They are not gods who have little need to communicate with policy makers; a bit of ideological impurity will not destroy their role. Their role is to study the economy and to present their conclusions (derived from maintaining as outside a perspective as possible) and to argue their case to the public as strongly as they can. If the public accepts it, fine; if not, that is also fine. Their work is simply one input into the decision-making process; it is not the final pronouncement. Recognizing this more limited role for economists is humbling for them, but it also frees them to take a more active direct role in policy formation without their current excessive concern that they might include some of their own value judgments in their prescriptions.

The Problem with an Outside Perspective

The problem of taking an outside perspective can be seen in economists' thinking about the economy. Taking an outside perspective, one is godlike and is led inevitably to one of two positions: that one should keep one's hands off society—laissez-faire—or that one should change society because one knows best. Both these positions are mistaken and do not capture the role economists should be playing in society.

Liberal economists have been willing to argue, generally implicitly, that they know best. Logically, this position cannot be held simultaneously with the position that individuals are rational and know best, but liberal economists do not push economic logic to extremes. They find room for new ideas and policy initiatives in economics even while using both the assumption of individual rationality and an "outside" perspective. But they can do so only by making logical jumps that conservatives delight in pointing out.

A few, generally conservative, economists push economic logic to extremes and arrive at the conclusion that there is no room for economic policy. Examples of this reasoning pervade economics; they include some versions of the invisible hand theorem, aspects of the public choice literature, the Coase theorem, New Classical economics, and the efficient market hypothesis. What all these arguments have in common is that they lead to a laissez-faire policy prescription because economists begin with an assumption that individuals are rational and that whenever they can make a gain from trade they will. Economists then ask what possible role there might be for government intervention that would make everyone better off than they would be on their own. Because any action worth doing would already have been done by rational individuals, given the assumption, the laissez-faire conclusion is preordained.

Now, I am not arguing that government intervention is good and laissez-faire bad. I am simply arguing that the laissez-faire conclusions and all the theorems and arguments associated with them are tautologically correct if the judge is viewing society from an "outside" perspective. They are also irrelevant. The arguments state no more than "what is, is."

To see why the outside perspective is wrong, consider a similar problem of perspective in making judgments about the ecological system. The ecological system is evolving. What role should humankind play in that evolution? The "outside" perspective places humankind outside of nature. From this outside perspective, if an animal or plant changes the environment, that is as it should be—nature's way. If humans change the environment—say, by devising a new chemical process—that is unnatural and, by implication, bad.

On a logical level, why should humans' actions be any less "natural" than animals' actions? If humans are unnatural, they have been unnatural forever, and their actions, including domestication of plants and animals, agriculture, reading, and thinking, are unnatural. But were humans not to have taken such actions, society would not be what it is, and what we are calling natural would not exist. Relying on natural-unnatural categorization places humankind outside of nature when, in fact, men and women and their ways of dealing with life are as much a part of natural processes (whatever they are) as are animal, vegetable, and physical operations.

In order to undertake policy, actions must be divided into good actions and bad actions, but the division is not synonymous with the natural/unnatural division. All policy actions that humans suggest are not unnatural and therefore bad, but that is the logical conclusion which one inevitably arrives at if we use the "outside" rather than the "inside" perspective.

Because economists take an outside perspective, that same natural/unnatural dichotomy pervades economic terminology. They use terms such as "the natural rate of interest" and "the natural rate of unemployment" in much the same way that people use the term "natural food": as a way to convey that the phenomenon is as it should be. But just as is the case with ecology, the separation of actions into two sets, natural and unnatural, is not a helpful way of looking at society.

I am not arguing that the outside perspective should not be the economists'. I am simply arguing that in their analysis they must remember that they ultimately remain inside the economic system. Having decided what is best from their attempt at taking an outside perspective, they must play an inside role in implementing their proposals, convincing others that their policy proposals are good for society. Doing so is as much a part of the economists' function as providing an understanding of the economy. Unless economists convince society that their policy recommendations arc best, their policy recommendations are not best. Economists cannot stand on any moral higher ground. Their ideas are as subject to the intellectual marketplace as lawyers' and politicians'.

The inside perspective avoids the logical problems of suggesting policy changes from an outside perspective. It answers the question of how, if individuals are doing everything in their power to make themselves as well off as possible, a policy implemented by government could make people better off. From an inside perspective, laissez-faire policies cannot be deductively arrived at from the model. If laissez-faire were optimal, society would not have designated a group of people—economists—to study how to improve the economy. One might conclude that a laissez-faire policy is preferable, but it is a conclusion to be arrived at in comparison with other policies; it is not a priori.

From within, economists cannot say, on the basis of what is natural (or efficient) and what is not, ''The government should, or should not, intervene.'' ''This policy should be introduced.'' ''This policy should not.'' In making judgments from an inside perspective, these criteria no longer pertain; there are no outside criteria to judge by. Efficiency is no longer an end in itself; it is simply one attribute of a policy that economists can use to convince policy makers of its desirability. Instead of stating that ''This policy is best because it is more efficient,'' their arguments for a policy will be on the basis of the policy's effect on society. Their arguments will be more like: ''This policy will change society this way.'' ''Here is what society will be like with this policy." "Here is what society will be like without this policy." Their arguments will include all aspects of a policy, including income distribution effects, administrative costs, and political feasibility.

Conclusion

Learning how to play this inside role would change the nature of economic education. Students would learn how to argue, how to write, and how to make contextual, as well as noncontextual, arguments. They would learn how to explain their ideas, how to modify theoretical notions, and how to make them fit into the political and social realities. Similarly, the research economists do would change, and the pure research about the "important" questions would be supplemented by the research about the "unimportant" questions, such as what policy real-world firms or governments should undertake.

Changing the perspective will not make economists more important than garbagemen. Garbagemen are naturally more important than most other groups in society. The change will, however, play a role in increasing economists' direct impact on society, not to the level of lawyers (God help us [society] that should happen), but perhaps to the level of doctors or dentists. Keynes once said, "If some day we could manage to get ourselves thought of as humble, competent people, on a level with dentists, that would be splendid." Changing to an inside perspective would be one small step for humility and competence. Whether that step will make society better off is debatable, but it will make economics a more meaningful profession.

Notes

1. No value judgments are being made here about what type of role a group should play. Shakespeare may have been right: Society might be better off if lawyers played no role. My point is simply that if lawyers were eliminated, it would have an immediate effect on the economy; if economists were eliminated, it would not.

2. If an individual can argue to his boss that he relied upon the best (interpret "most expensive") advice, he cannot be blamed when things go wrong.

3. In a survey of graduate students that Arjo Klamer and I did (see "The Making of an Economist," p. 47), 3 percent of the students thought institutional knowledge was very important to getting on the fast track in economics; 68 percent thought it unimportant.

4. When Robert Lucas, a top theoretical macroeconomist, was asked what he would do if appointed chairman of the Council of Economic Advisors, he quipped, "I would resign."

2

The Best as the Enemy
of the Good

I was recently ranting and raving to a fellow economist (who has been very successful) about the problems in the economics profession, something that I do relatively frequently. She listened and told me she agreed completely with me. She said that much of what economists did was a waste of time. However, she was not as concerned as I. She said that the difference between my view and her view was that I thought there was something that economists should be doing that they're not and that I cared. She didn't care because even though economists weren't doing much good, at least, by being irrelevant, they weren't doing much bad.

She was perceptive in recognizing that my criticism of the profession is based on a strong belief in economics. I criticize economics because I believe in economics; I believe that economists have done, and can do, much good in the world. Good economists help people see how desired goals can be realistically achieved. It's because of that potential for doing good that I become so upset when I see the potential being wasted.

In textbook economics doing good isn't what economics is about; according to the texts doing good involves value judgments and therefore belongs to normative economics, whereas, according to the textbooks, economists do positive economics which is not concerned with value judgments and hence is not concerned with doing good. According to most texts, positive economics avoids value judgments, and economics that does not avoid value judgments is normative economics. Luckily, many economists don't take the textbook prescriptions seriously, and economists as a group do a lot of good. Economists help prevent special interest groups from taking over government; they point out rip-offs by business; they give some logic and form to the tax system; they fight monopolization in all its forms; they help the economy operate more smoothly than it otherwise would; and they help design policies that make the economy fairer.

These statements and all the activities they describe involve value judgments, as any policy prescription must. According to the textbook definition of positive economics, economics has nothing to say about policy. The textbooks are wrong. "Involving value judgments" does not make an activity normative. Normative economics is economics with hidden value judgments. Positive economics is economics with the value judgments presented as openly as possible. In deciding whether economics is normative or positive, the relevant questions are: Whose normative judgments are they? and How clearly are those value judgments made? If the value judgments are hidden and obscured, then the analysis is normatively tainted, not because it involves value judgments but only because it hides those value judgments. If, however, those value judgments are clearly stated and the analysis is posed: "To achieve these ends these are the policies you should follow," the analysis is not normatively tainted. It is positive analysis at its best.

My distinction is hardly novel; it was nicely outlined in Gunnar Myrdal's writings on political economy in the 1930s. But somehow in economists' quest to be ideologically pure, that distinction has been obscured. In a misplaced attempt at ideological purity—to avoid any value judgments that anyone might object to—economists and the preponderance of economic theory have come to focus on a single criterion—Pareto efficiency—technically defined as a state in which all people cannot be made better off without at least one person being made worse off. According to the texts, the only policies the "best" economists can recommend, while doing positive economics, are Pareto-optimal policies. And that's what's wrong with the "best" economists. In their attempt to be pure, they've made themselves irrelevant. What is ironic is that even in pure theory, the pursuit of Pareto optimality is problematic, as Amartya Sen (1970) has nicely shown. But in the real world it is worse than problematic. It is ludicrous. It limits the set of real-world policies economists can recommend to the null set, since the repercussions of any real-world policy inevitably hurt someone.

The goal of Pareto optimality is like Howard Hughes's approach to cleanliness. It is obsessive and irrational and leads to holing up in a hotel room, cut off from the real world, which might contaminate one with germs. In the futile search to avoid germs, you give up living. You pass up the good in your search for the best.

But my argument against what the textbooks tell economists to do is stronger than that it directs them to irrelevancy. Real-world positive economics tells people how to achieve real-world goals. Since Pareto optimality is not the criterion most people use in judging the normative implications of a policy, using Pareto optimality as a goal is not doing good positive economics. It is not telling people how to achieve their goals—goals that involve distributional, transitional equity, and fairness questions. Since textbook positive economics is not telling people how to achieve their goals, it is lousy economics. Much of what the textbooks put forward as positive economics is more like mental masturbation, which may be enjoyable when done behind closed doors but is not something one should do in public (a normative judgment).

If people knew what they wanted and could match their real-world desires with achievable goals, the economist's job would be similar to an engineer's. Economists would state: To achieve goal x, do y. The normative questions would be similar to the normative question faced by any engineer who finds the goals given him or her repulsive. That is a question of a different level which reflects the fact that positive economics is not necessarily about doing good; it is about achieving goals. If the goals aren't good, then efficiency—achieving those goals in the best way possible—isn't good. Efficiency only has meaning in achieving stated goals.

But the role of an economist is not as simple as the engineer's, since people often don't have well-defined goals. No one comes and tells an economist, "I want a bridge that will carry at least 40,000 pounds." The decision makers asking advice of economists generally aren't exactly sure what their goals are, and the goals they think they have are often laden with inconsistencies. These people are the equivalent of a medical doctor's patient who says he wants to live to be 190, eat anything he wants, and run a 3-minute, 40-second mile at age 110. Faced with such patients, I suspect medical doctors would have also retreated to writing irrelevant articles about Pareto-optimal health—leaving the patient to fend for himself.

In short, efficiency is not an end in itself. Efficiency has meaning only in reference to goals. Efficiency is a description of how one achieves one's goals. Thus, without specifying the realistic goals of a policy, economists can't talk about efficiency and can't do good positive economics.

Doing Good Economics

Before an economist can do positive economics, someone must help the decision makers understand precisely what their goals are and what is and is not achievable. This counseling role is necessary, and if no one else fulfills it, the economist must, before he or she can do the job of a positive economist.

Maintaining objectivity in counseling is enormously difficult; the counselor must be able to separate out his or her normative judgments from policies and help the decision makers see what is, or isn't, a realistic goal. Such economic counseling is a necessary part of good economics because people often fail to differentiate the technical problems of certain policy proposals from the normative judgments embodied in policy proposals. In such cases, it is economists' first role to help people see the distinction.

Let's consider an example on which most economists agree: tariffs. Most economists oppose tariffs. But good economists don't oppose tariffs because they are Pareto-inoptimal; removing tariffs will make some people better off and some people worse off. Good economists oppose tariffs because they believe tariffs are inconsistent with the true goals of society. Generally tariffs do not achieve the goals society has: fairness and equity. But despite their speaking with one voice on the issue, economists have not had the influence on tariffs that they might if they would relate their opposition to tariffs to society's goals and spend more time counseling decision makers and providing insight into why tariffs don't meet society's goals.

Another example is the minimum wage; most economists oppose the minimum wage, but not because it is Pareto-inoptimal. They oppose it because they don't believe it achieves society's ends. Economic counseling would lead a person through the economists' argument against the minimum wage: So, you like the minimum wage? Why do you like it? Is it because it gets income to individuals who need it? So it's not the minimum wage you like; it's getting income to those who need it? What do you mean: "need it"? Do the unemployed need it? The unemployed, you know, won't be helped by a minimum wage. In fact, more people will become unemployed because of a minimum wage. What if there were another policy that could perform better in getting money to more of those who you believe need it? Would you prefer that policy? Why or why not?

By such reasoning an economist can help people see what their normative judgments are and how the desired goals might be reached by alternative policies that cost less—i.e., that achieve the desired goal—more efficiently. That's what good economists do. Good positive economists show people how to achieve their goals more effectively, and to do that it is necessary to help people define their goals.

The best economists eschew such activities as normative, beneath their dignity. But such a position confines the best economists to practical irrelevance. Telling pretend people how they can use pretend policies to reach unrealistic goals is what the "best" economics is designed to do.

So-called conservative economists have well understood the advantage of the good over the best. They have made people reexamine their goals and have practiced "good" economics rather than the "best" economics. For example, Milton Friedman, through a series of policy suggestions, has forced people to look at their actual normative views. His work on the role of licensure and regulation is a good example. His argument for his proposed policies is not that they are Pareto-optimal; it is that his proposals achieve normative goals of fairness that most people subscribe to.

Another example of good economics is the public choice school. Its members have played an enormously beneficial role in challenging the view that government tries to do good and in forcing economics to look at the policies that actually get implemented, rather than the policies economists recommend.

Both Friedman and the public choice school are generally classified as conservative economists. I'm generally classified as a liberal economist, in part because I often criticize the conservative economists. But my criticism of them is grounded in the same sensibility that leads me to rant and rave about the profession: They're doing good, but they could do better. Their policy proposals are based on often unstated normative judgments that they believe most people hold. I believe they are often right about those unstated normative judgments. If they'd argue for them that way, I'd likely support them. But they don't. They often argue as if theirs is the only logical position and that it is not a normative view. But that isn't so.

It is always possible that they have misperceived people's normative views; for example, it is always possible that people like a policy because they like the policy, not because of what that policy achieves. When people like a policy for itself, and not for what it achieves, economists can't say the policy is bad. People's goals are the policy. But generally, in my view, people are confused about their goals. Conservative economists could do enormous good in helping decision makers overcome this confusion, but instead they simply strengthen decision makers' inconsistencies, all the while pretending that the conservative economists' policy is not normative. I believe that many of the policies advocated by Milton Friedman and the public choice school can be defended as the policies that the majority of society would choose if society understood its underlying values and the way real-world policies are implemented. They are policies that achieve fairness as most people interpret fairness. Other policies, in my view, cannot be so defended, but discussions of what can and cannot be defended have not filled the pages of economics journals. Instead economic journals concentrate on discussions of whether policies are or are not Pareto-efficient in a make-believe model of a make-believe world.

Whenever one tries to define society's underlying values, one can make mistakes; one can confuse one's own view with what one believes society's view is and be guilty of crossing over the line that separates normative from positive economics. Good economists walk precariously close to that line, relying on other good economists to tell them when they step over. If one stays away from that line, as the "best" economists do, one condemns one's work to irrelevancy. The "best" economists have become like judges who refuse to discuss real-world cases because if they decided real-world cases they might make a mistake. Striving for the "best" is the enemy of the good.

2

Economics, Institutions, and Methodology

3

The Making of
an Economist

As economists, we have an interest in and individual knowledge of the initiation process that turns students into professional economists. However, other than anecdotal evidence, very little in the way of data exists. This paper is a step toward providing insight into that process.

There are differing opinions about graduate economic education; most are privately expressed. However, some do surface, usually the most critical. For example, Robert Kuttner (1985), summarizing the views of critical economists such as Wassily Leontief and John Kenneth Galbraith, writes: "Departments of economics are graduating a generation of *idiots savants*, brilliant at esoteric mathematics yet innocent of actual economic life." Our study of graduate education provides some data to help in assessing such views.

Besides being of general interest, information on the making of economists is important to the sociological and rhetorical approach to economic methodology (Coats 1985; Klamer 1983; McCloskey 1986; Whitley 1984). The graduate school experi-

This essay was written jointly with Arjo Klamer. We would like to thank Caroline Craven, Lee Cuba, Marion Just, Chrystal Sharp, Stephen Smith, and the students of the various economics departments who filled in the surveys and participated in the conversations. For helpful comments on early drafts of this manuscript we would like to thank Bob Coats, Fred Dirks, Rendigs Fels, David Lindauer, and Robert Solow.

ence plays an important role in determining economic discourse; it certifies economists as professionals; it establishes economists' view of argumentation and guides them as to what is important to study and what is not. To understand economic discourse one should have a good sense of the professionalization of economists that occurs in graduate school.

We obtained our data from questionnaires distributed to graduate students at six top-ranking graduate economic programs— University of Chicago, Columbia University, Harvard University, Massachusetts Institute of Technology, Stanford University, and Yale University—exploring who current graduate students are and what they think about economics, the economy, and graduate school. The 212 respondents were relatively equally divided by year of study. (See Appendix for a discussion of the questionnaire and methodology.) We followed up our survey with a series of interviews.

We present the information gained from the questionnaire in four sections, keeping our editorial discussion to a minimum. Thorough discussion of the issues raised by this survey is beyond the scope of a journal article. In a final section, however, we do provide some of our interpretations.

Profile of Students

The typical graduate student in economics at these selected institutions is a twenty-six-year-old, middle-class, nonreligious white male who is involved in a long-term relationship. (In our sample 18.9 percent were female; there was one Hispanic, and there were no Blacks.) Most had attended highly competitive undergraduate colleges and came from relatively well-to-do families. More than half (54 percent) of their fathers had advanced degrees, 23 percent of the mothers had advanced degrees, and the average family income was approximately $50,000. Eighty-seven percent majored or concentrated in economics as undergraduates, 28 percent in mathematics, 24 percent in other social sciences, 15 percent in the humanities, and 9 percent in the natural sciences. (Students could have both a major and a concentration.) For most students (63 percent) graduate work in economics was their only choice of career when they applied. Those who contemplated alternatives considered policy-related work or law school. Part of the reason for such clear focus is that 50 percent of the students had worked, traveled, or studied in another graduate field before they began their economics graduate program.

George Stigler (1982, first published 1975) has remarked that economics tends to make individuals conservative. At least at this stage of their careers that was not the case with our respondents. In terms of political views, 47 percent considered themselves liberal, 22 percent moderate, 15 percent conservative, and 12 percent radical. (Four percent were "other.") Thus, at least for students at the top schools, the majority see themselves as predominantly liberal.

Interests of Students

When asked an open question as to what they most liked and disliked about graduate school, 36 percent stated that they most liked the intellectual environment and 24 percent said they liked the courses and research. As to the things they liked least, the majority of comments focused on the heavy load of mathematics and theory and a lack of relevance of the material they were learning. Whatever their reservations, only 6 percent said they would definitely not do it again; 21 percent were unsure.[1]

In terms of future jobs, 53 percent were planning to pursue an academic career, 33 percent were planning to go into policy-related work, 17 percent into business, 8 percent into research institutions, and 2 percent into journalism.[2] These results are roughly consistent with an unpublished study by the National Science Foundation (reported in the *Committee on the Status of Women in the Economics Profession March 1987 Newsletter*, p. 4), which found that 60 percent of all new economics Ph.D.'s plan to enter academia. Our lower percentage may be accounted for by the difference in the sampled populations: graduate students vs. new Ph.D.'s. The difference would then suggest that students not planning to enter academia are more likely to drop out.

The academic jobs the students desired were primarily at research universities. Forty-one percent wanted to be at a major university in fifteen years, 32 percent at a policy-oriented research institution, 16 percent at a good liberal arts college, 11 percent at a major research institute, and 9 percent in the private sector. The students confirmed these preferences in the interviews. As one student said: "That's definitely not the thing to do—to walk into [a well-known professor's] office and announce that you want to teach at [a major liberal arts college]."

Not all of the 53 percent had academia on their minds when they entered. In our conversations several students referred to peer pressure and the opinion of their professors as important factors in their decisions. When alternatives to a career at a major institution came up in conversation among fourth-year students, the students emphasized the problems. One student noted:

> It is very hard [to go into a public policy job] when a lot of friends, and certainly the faculty, are judging you by how good a job you get. When you want to succeed in their eyes you get a job at a major university. It is very hard to chuck all this and be a failure in the eyes of all those people who have been very important in the last four years.

If graduate schools are graduating *idiots savants* who have no interest in policy, it is not because students enter graduate school with no interest. The majority of students (53 percent) considered a desire to engage in policy formation very important in their decision to attend graduate school; only 17 percent considered such a desire unimportant. The other significant reason for attending graduate school was enjoyment of their undergraduate major in economics (53 percent); 13 percent considered that unimportant. During graduate school 71 percent worked as teaching or research assistants, 11 percent worked as consultants, and 11

Table 1

The Importance of Reading in Other Fields

	Very important	Important	Moderately important	Unimportant
Mathematics	41	32	21	6
History	34	34	24	8
Political science	24	30	33	13
Sociology	16	29	35	21
Philosophy	15	27	27	15
Psychology	9	20	44	27
Computer science	8	26	35	30
Physics	2	6	27	64

percent did political work. (Some students did more than one kind of work.) Thirty-four percent were already in the process of writing scholarly papers for publication.

In the survey as well as in our conversations, concern with the relevance of economics dominated. When asked what the major factor in their choice of dissertation topic was, or would be, there was a focus on wanting to do relevant work. When asked about the factors that influence the choice of dissertation, the majority (67 percent) stated that they wanted to understand some economic phenomenon. Seventeen percent said that getting the dissertation done was an important reason, while 4 percent mentioned the applicability of certain mathematical or econometric techniques.

Jacob Viner once said that "men are not narrow in their intellectual interest by nature; it takes special and rigorous training to accomplish that end." Based on our survey we can conclude that graduate economics education is succeeding in narrowing students' interests. Most of the respondents had wide interests, but class work left little time to follow up these other interests. We asked them how important to their development as economists readings in various fields would be; their responses are shown in Table 1. Even though most graduate students believed that reading in areas such as history and political science and, to a lesser extent, sociology and philosophy, was important for their

Table 2

Interest of Students by Area

Area	Great interest	Moderate interest	No interest
Macro	42.6	43.5	13.9
Political economy	36.1	38.0	25.5
Micro	35.7	48.3	15.9
International	30.5	43.8	25.7
Industrial organization	30.1	45.1	24.8
Money and banking	28.0	41.1	30.9
Development	26.0	42.3	31.7
Labor	24.6	40.1	35.3
Econometrics	22.4	55.7	21.9
Public finance	18.9	47.6	30.5
History of thought	18.7	50.2	30.6
Law and economics	10.6	40.1	47.3
Comparative	9.3	42.4	48.6
Urban	5.4	27.0	67.6

development as economists, we found from our interviews that most did not undertake such reading because they lacked the time.

Another indication of the narrowing process is that students also felt that graduate school gave them little opportunity for interdisciplinary discussions. Even though 60 percent said they had frequent interactions with students or scholars in other disciplines, only 13 percent thought those interactions intellectual.

The interest of our respondents (ranked by percentage of students having great interest) are given in Table 2. In terms of interest among areas within economics, our respondents mirrored a hierarchy that Benjamin Ward (1972) argued exists, although there were some notable exceptions.[3] Microeconomics and macroeconomics coincide with Ward's suggested hierarchy of the profession. Econometrics is lower but has a significant amount of moderate interest. Economic development and industrial organization ranked higher than Ward suggested they would. Political economy (not found in Ward's classification) received significant interest. (Political economy would include both neo-classical political economy, such as public choice, and Marxist political economy.)

Table 3

Perceptions of Success

	Very important	Moderately important	Unim- portant	Don't know
Being smart in the sense of being good at problem solving	65	32	3	1
Excellence in mathematics	57	41	2	0
Being very knowledgeable about one particular field	37	42	19	2
Ability to make connections with prominent professors	26	50	16	9
Being interested in, and good at, empirical research	16	60	23	1
Having a broad knowledge of the economics literature	10	41	43	5
Having a thorough knowledge of the economy	3	22	68	7

One of the objectives of our study was a better understanding of the perceptions of their discourse that students acquire in graduate school. For that reason, we asked them what abilities will likely place students on a fast track. That question provided some of the most dramatic results of our survey.[4] We presented students possible abilities, which they ranked as shown in Table 3.

Knowledge of the economy and knowledge of economic literature do not make an economist successful, according to graduate students. Forty-three percent believed that a knowledge of economic literature was unimportant, while only 10 percent felt that it was very important. Sixty-eight percent believed that a thorough knowledge about the economy was unimportant; only 3 percent believed it was very important. This attitude was confirmed in our interviews. The following typical comment was given in response to a question about what students thought of class work:

> One of the questions of your survey was: "What puts students on the fast track?" and if I remember correctly, one of the choices was

"general knowledge about the economy." You can walk in off the
street and take the courses and not know what the Fortune 500 is and
blaze through with flying colors. You can also come in and know the
difference between subordinated debentures and junk bonds and fail
miserably.

Clearly these results raise significant questions about the nature of graduate school, what is being taught, and the socialization process that occurs. The issues raised here are complicated
ones, but the results suggest that these issues need to be addressed by the profession.

In the questionnaire we did not ask whether students like
what they perceive in graduate school, nor are graduate students
necessarily the ones to ask. As Robert Solow stated when commenting on this paper, "To say that something is wrong with
graduate education is to say that something is wrong with the
economics profession."

For what it is worth, the interviews suggested a definite tension,
frustration, and cynicism that, in our view, went beyond the normal
graduate school blues. There was a strong sense that economics was
a game and that hard work in devising relevant models that demonstrated a deep understanding of institutions would have a lower
payoff than devising models that were analytically neat; the facade,
not the depth of knowledge, was important. This cynicism is not
limited to the graduate school experience but is applied also to the
state of the art as they perceive it. A fourth-year student stated:

> We go to the money workshop. You'd think that for edification the
> faculty brings in supposedly some of the best young people through-
> out the country to give macro talks about their current research. All
> of us go, week after week, and come back, and just laugh at them.
> Big reputations. Often because it's just very implausible, very com-
> plicated.

Differences between Graduate
Students and the Profession

Bruno Frey et al. (1984) recently surveyed the beliefs of American economists. Our questionnaire included questions similar to

Table 4

Economic Opinions of Graduate Students Compared to Frey Study of American Economists

	Graduate students				American economists		
	yes	yes but	no	not sure[a]	yes	yes but	no
Fiscal policy can be an effective tool in stabilizing policy.[b]	35	49	11	5	65	27	8
The FRB should maintain a constant money growth.	9	34	45	12	14	25	61
A minimum wage increases unemployment among young and unskilled workers.	34	39	18	9	68	22	10
Tariffs and import quotas reduce general economic welfare.	36	49	9	6	81	16	3
Inflation is primarily a monetary phenomenon.	27	33	29	11	27	30	43
Wage-price controls should be used to control inflation.	1	17	73	9	6	22	72
Worker democracy will increase labor productivity.	13	40	22	24	—	—	—
The market system tends to discriminate against women.	24	27	39	10	—	—	—
The capitalist system has an inherent tendency toward crisis.	8	23	59	13	—	—	—
The income distribution in developed nations should be more equal.	47	32	14	7	40	31	29

[a]The survey of Frey et al. did not allow the "not sure" option.
[b]The question as formulated in the Frey survey is: Does fiscal policy have a stimulative impact on a less than fully employed economy?

theirs, allowing us to compare their responses for American economists with ours for graduate students. Table 4 compares the two sets of results. As can be seen in this percentage comparison, graduate students tend to qualify their conclusions, especially about the role of quotas and tariffs and the effectiveness of fiscal policy, much more than do most American economists.

Distinctive Characteristics
of Graduate Programs

In an insightful study of the economics profession George Stigler and Claire Friedland (Stigler 1982) pose the question: "Are the major centers of graduate instruction in the U.S. 'schools' in the sense of leaving distinctive imprints upon their doctorates?" They examine the citation practices from 1950 to 1968 of economists who received their doctorates between 1950 and 1955. Stigler and Friedland find "genuine differences among the universities in the attention and respect paid to various scholars." But the differences are so small, according to them, that they do not provide evidence for the existence of divergent schools of economic thought.

Unlike the study by Stigler and Friedland, our survey does not cover research interests after graduate school, but it gives insight into the opinions that graduate students hold. The results shown in Table 5 demonstrate that graduate schools, particularly Stigler's own University of Chicago, have distinctive characters. For example, differences come out clearly in the answers to questions about economics as a science.

Looking at the "Total" column in Table 5, we see that the scientific status of economics is clearly in doubt among students. A majority deny two key elements of any objective science: the distinction between positive and normative economics and agreement on fundamental issues. However, those views are not evenly distributed among schools. For example, without MIT and Harvard, a small majority would conclude that economists do agree on fundamental issues.

Table 5

Opinions of Economics as a Science: Comparison among Schools

	Chicago	MIT	Harvard	Stanford	Columbia	Yale	Total
Neoclassical economics is relevant for the economic problems of today.							
strongly agree	69	31	20	34	24	33	34
agree somewhat	28	56	56	60	68	60	54
disagree	3	11	22	6	8	8	11
no clear opinion	0	2	2	0	0	0	1
Economists agree on fundamental issues.							
strongly agree	3	4	2	2	4	13	4
agree somewhat	47	31	27	51	48	33	40
disagree	44	60	68	43	44	47	52
no clear opinion	6	4	2	4	4	7	4
There is a sharp line between positive and normative economics.							
strongly agree	22	7	9	9	0	7	9
agree somewhat	38	16	4	30	32	33	23
disagree	34	73	84	55	52	60	62
no clear opinion	6	4	2	6	16	0	6
Economics is the most scientific social science.							
strongly agree	47	27	9	27	36	13	28
agree somewhat	28	36	43	31	24	47	39
disagree	9	24	30	23	28	40	19
no clear opinion	16	13	18	19	12	0	14

The response indicates that Chicago students are most convinced of the relevance of neo-classical economics, and Harvard students least convinced. Apart from the Chicago students, the majority of graduate students question the possibility of separating positive and normative economics. In fact, three-quarters of those at MIT and five-sixths of those at Harvard deny the distinction between positive and normative economics. Chicago accepts it; other schools have bare majorities against.

The differences among schools are brought out more clearly when we compare the opinions of students at various schools on economic perspectives in Table 6 and on the importance of eco-

Table 6

Economic Opinions: A Comparison among Schools

	Chicago	MIT	Harvard	Stanford	Columbia	Yale
Fiscal policy can be an effective tool in stabilizing policy.						
strongly agree	6	48	30	30	54	60
agree with reservations	34	51	65	52	38	33
disagree	44	0	2	9	8	7
no clear opinion	16	2	2	9	0	0
The Fed should maintain a constant growth of the money supply.						
agree	41	0	7	2	4	0
agree with reservations	44	27	24	39	50	21
disagree	9	60	57	44	33	64
no clear opinion	6	13	11	15	13	14
A minimum wage increases unemployment among young and unskilled workers.						
agree	70	24	15	36	38	33
agree with reservations	28	53	41	40	25	27
disagree	3	11	35	19	21	13
no clear opinion	0	11	9	4	9	27
Tariffs and import quotas reduce general economic welfare.						
agree	66	38	20	32	38	33
agree with reservations	34	42	56	51	54	60
disagree	0	13	11	9	8	7
no clear opinion	0	4	13	9	0	0
Inflation is primarily a monetary phenomenon.						
agree	84	7	15	23	29	13
agree with reservations	16	44	26	45	25	40
disagree	0	36	46	23	33	33
no clear opinion	0	11	11	10	13	13
The market system tends to discriminate against women.						
agree	6	24	44	11	38	27
agree with reservations	19	22	20	38	21	53
disagree	69	40	26	43	33	13
no clear opinion	3	13	11	9	8	7
The distribution of income in developed nations should be more equal.						
agree	16	52	54	52	46	60
agree with reservations	50	30	33	24	37	20
disagree	19	9	13	17	9	20
no clear opinion	15	9	0	7	9	7

nomic assumptions in Table 7. These two tables strongly support the hypothesis that Chicago constitutes a "school" that is distinct from other schools. It seems to be a creed at Chicago that inflation is primarily a monetary phenomenon, with 100 percent agreeing with the proposition. At Harvard, 46 percent disagree. Likewise, it seems a creed at MIT that fiscal policy can be an effective tool for stabilization, with no student disagreeing. At Chicago, 44 percent disagree.

The differences are also significant in the responses to the microeconomic questions. Chicago students have a significantly higher degree of confidence in the market than students at other schools. Harvard shows most variety in the answers with a significant number of the students skeptical of the market.

The "Total" column in Table 7 shows that most graduate students found the rationality assumption important but were cautious about the rational expectations hypothesis. Only 17 percent considered the hypothesis very important, while 25 percent considered it unimportant. The assumption of imperfect competition and the assumption of behavior according to conventions ranked higher than the rational expectations assumptions.

Looking at the breakdown among schools, we see that Chicago students, compared with students in other schools, demonstrate the greatest commitment to neo-classical economics, with significant support for the rational expectations hypothesis and relatively less interest in the assumptions of price rigidity, imperfect competition, and cost mark-up pricing. (One could also say that other schools demonstrate little support for Chicago ideas. As one third-year MIT student noted: "There are no Lucas types [at MIT].") It is particularly striking that not a single MIT student thinks the rational expectations assumption is very important.

Chicago was unique in other areas as well. For example, only 19 percent of the Chicago students perceive a significant tension between their course work and their interests. This number contrasts with an average of 42 percent for the other schools. No stress is reported by 60 percent at Chicago, compared with an average of 28 percent at other schools.

Table 7

Importance of Economic Assumptions

	Chicago	Harvard	MIT	Stanford	Total
Rationality assumptions					
very important	78	35	44	58	51
important in some cases	22	51	44	36	41
unimportant	0	14	9	6	7
no strong opinion	0	0	0	0	1
Rational expectations					
very important	59	14	0	9	17
important in some cases	38	45	71	53	53
unimportant	0	38	18	32	25
no strong opinion	3	2	7	6	5
Price rigidities					
very important	6	37	38	26	27
important in some cases	56	54	56	65	60
unimportant	38	7	4	4	10
no strong opinion	0	2	0	4	3
Imperfect competition					
very important	16	47	51	38	40
important in some cases	72	47	44	60	55
unimportant	9	7	0	2	4
no strong opinion	3	0	2	0	2
Cost mark-up pricing					
very important	0	7	9	11	9
important in some cases	16	48	62	41	46
unimportant	50	26	18	33	26
no strong opinion	34	19	9	15	18
Behavior according to con-ventions					
very important	0	16	18	4	4
important in some cases	31	55	69	64	25
unimportant	31	9	2	4	57
no strong opinion	38	20	11	28	15

While Chicago definitely constitutes a specific school, there is less, but nonetheless some, evidence that other programs do, too. Were we to generalize, we would say that Harvard students appear to be most skeptical, while Stanford students place themselves in the spectrum of opinions between Chicago and MIT students.

The fact that Chicago represents a different school does not mean that the school shapes the students to its image. The students could have been self-selected. We tested this possibility in two ways. First, we asked students to compare their beliefs before graduate school with their beliefs now in regard to certain issues such as the relevance of neo-classical economics, whether a sharp line can be drawn between positive and normative economics, and whether economics is the most scientific of the social sciences. No clear-cut conclusion emerged from these questions. Approximately 50 percent of the students felt that they had not changed their minds in graduate school. Among those who did change their minds, for the total sample of all schools there was no clear-cut movement toward or away from the beliefs associated with that school.

Looking at the data by school, however, one can detect a slight pattern, especially at Chicago. For example, at Chicago 44 percent did not change their view about the relevance of neo-classical economics from what it was before graduate school. The 56 percent who did change their minds were divided as follows: 3 percent thought it less relevant and 53 percent thought it more relevant. This is in direct contrast to other schools. For example, at MIT 62 percent of the students believed that they did not change their view of the relevance of neo-classical economics from what it was before graduate school, but those who did change their mind were split: 22 percent thought neo-classical economics more relevant; 16 percent thought it less relevant.

Another example can be seen in students' beliefs about how scientific economics is. Forty-seven percent of the Chicago students did not change their minds: 34 percent thought economics more scientific; 19 percent thought it less scientific. These data suggest that schools tend to reinforce previously held opinions.

Although we did not ask questions about previous beliefs on economic policy, we were able to separate answers to questions by year of study and thereby capture changes in views that occurred after the first year. This provided a second test, although the results of this test are inconclusive because the study was done in the spring and it is possible that first-year students could have already been influenced by the school. Still, this test also suggests that self-selection is important but that some adjustment and reinforcement of views occurs at graduate school. For example, at MIT 66 percent of first- and second-year students agreed that inflation was a monetary phenomenon, whereas only 42 percent of fourth- and fifth-year students agreed. (At Chicago 100 percent agreed in all years.) But the comparison also presented some anomalies. For example, at Harvard 26 percent of first- and second-year students felt that inflation was primarily a monetary phenomenon; while 53 percent of fourth- and fifth-year students believed that it was.

Answers to the two other questions provide a good sense of the reinforcement of views that occurs in graduate school: 58 percent of first- and second-year Chicago students believed that fiscal policy could be effective, but only 36 percent of the fourth- and fifth-year students believed that it was. At Harvard and MIT all but one student in all years agreed that fiscal policy is effective. In response to a question about the minimum wage, all Chicago students in all years believed it increased unemployment; of Harvard students in the first and second year 45 percent disagreed; in the fourth and fifth year only 24 percent disagreed.

Our conclusion from these two incomplete tests is that while some adjusting to the school view does occur in graduate school, unless the changes occur in the first year, the predominant factor in determining the beliefs of a graduate school student is self-selection. Graduate schools modify those beliefs somewhat but often reinforce previously existing views.

Some Thoughts about the Implications

Reporting the data is one thing; interpreting them is another. We were especially struck by a series of tensions that emerged in the making of economists. Graduate students are interested in policy; most entered economics because they hoped it would shed light on policy. In the early years when they learn techniques and basic skills, the application to policy is limited, and this causes some frustration for the students, as shown in the following conversations:

Student 1: It seems to me that we spent six weeks in the macroeconomics course where we did a lot of algebra, we took a lot of derivatives, but we never really talked about how applicable these models were, how reasonable these assumptions were.

Student 2: I don't think we get policy at all in our courses. Well, there's Theory of Commercial Policy, but we don't really get policy in that. We get, "What's the optimum tariff?"

Some students argued for the advantage of specializing in technique. Other students disagreed, as can be seen in the following exchange:

Student 3: I think there are two things going on. One is the first year we're getting equipped [with the basics]. I think it's very important to make sure that we cover an agenda of items. And I think there's another feeling—I've seen this in a quote that Solow had—that policy is sort of for simpletons. If you really know your theory, the policy implications are pretty straightforward. It's not really the really challenging meat and potato stuff for a really sharp theorist. I think that's another reason why they don't spend much time on applications.[5]

Student 4: Not necessarily. I feel like the implementation of policy is a much trickier question than those people give it credit for. A guy like [names an instructor], for instance, on the faculty here, is very concerned with that sort of thing, and I get the impression that he's almost sneered at for caring about practical problems that come along with implementing theoretical results. And there really are very few people on the faculty whose work I've seen who really take that sort of thing into consideration.

The other students agreed.

To make it through the first two years of graduate school, students have to focus on technique. Thus, the graduates are well trained in problem solving, but it is technical problem-solving which has more to do with formal modeling techniques than with real-world problems. To do the problems little real-world knowledge of institutions is needed, and in many cases such knowledge would actually be a hindrance since the simplifying assumptions would be harder to accept.

Students come into graduate school wanting economics to be

relevant and are taught theory and techniques that point out the complexity of the problems. But they quickly come around; they perceive the incentives in the system. They are convinced that formal modeling is important to success but are not convinced that the formal models provide deep insight into, or reflect a solid understanding of, the economic institutions being modeled. Believing this, they want to be trained in what the profession values. Thus we find that students who believe they are not being taught the most complicated theory feel deprived and unhappy because they worry about the ability to compete.

The value students place on learning technique can be seen clearly in the interviews with students at Columbia. In response to a question about how they and the faculty would respond to bringing in a higher level of theoretical economists, they stated:

> *Student 1:* If you ask me, that's [the absence of a high-level theoretical economist] one of the weaknesses of Columbia when we go into the job market. We don't have a high level theorist here.
> *Student 2:* What do you mean—like pure money theory?
> *Student 1:* In micro. Micro theorists, topology—we don't have anyone like that here. We don't touch it.
> *Questioner:* Does that bother you?
> *Student 3:* Yes, it worries me greatly. Because I'm interested in micro theory, that's what I want to do.
> *Student 1:* It's a liability not to understand foundations.
> *Student 2:* And I kind of think that math for math's sake is nice, just to learn the math, and that it's a good way of thinking. And then maybe some of it might be relevant to economic ideas.

The likely reason for students' transformation into technique-oriented individuals is that most of them aspire to academic jobs. They know that tenure depends on publication in the right journals. They logically choose a source of study that is most likely to lead to their goal of succeeding in that intermediate goal. Knowing a technique that can be applied to various areas can lead to five or ten articles; knowing a specific area well might lead to one or two articles. Thus, students see little incentive to know the literature in an area or to have institutional knowledge of a particular area. This emphasis does not reflect their lack of concern about policy; it reflects the perceived incentives in the system. Novelty in approach, not slogging through enormous amounts of data or becoming an expert in the literature, is important.

Conclusion

We are not saying that graduate education in economics is bad or good. We arc merely stating how students perceive the incentives and providing a possible explanation for why those incentives exist. If we are correct in our explanation, these incentives are the inevitable result of other aspects of the economics profession that we have not considered here. The lack of policy relevance of economic theory is not because of a lack of interest in policy by students. Thus, it seems that some very real socialization process is going on. In our conversations the students frequently brought up the subject themselves, often using the notion of socialization:

Student 1 (a fourth-year student): I came into economics with little economics and math and felt very much that I was being socialized into something, and put through a wringer of linear algebra. After the first two years it has been fabulous. The thesis-writing process has been really fun.

Student 2 (a first-year student): The first year seems to shape the rest of our career as an economist. It is really disturbing. We are moving into something but nobody really knows what that is, except that they were socialized in this way of thinking by people who got their Ph.D.'s five years ago. It's like being brainwashed. You are deprived of sleep. You are subjected to extreme stress, bombarded with contradictory notions, and you end up accepting anything.

Student 3 (another fourth-year student): I feel that I have been socialized into the profession, into its way of thinking. When I came here I would have sworn that I was to go straight into political work. I was reasonably skeptical of these hoity-toity articles in academic journals where the thing to do is to get an academic position, write papers for journals, and the idea is that those who can't do economics do policy. ("Or teach at a liberal arts school," added another student.) Now the research side is more valuable, or maybe it is that I view that as the thing I am supposed to be doing.

Others present confirmed this experience.

Our attempt in this paper was to provide some empirical data that allow us better to understand the process that shapes economists. Certain results seem unambiguous and worth repeating. Specifically, there is a significant variety of opinions among graduate economics students and among the schools in the survey, and there definitely seems to be a Chicago school of economics. There are also tensions between the emphasis on techniques and the desire to do policy-oriented work. What students believe leads to success in graduate school is definitely techniques; success has little to do with understanding the economy, nor does it have much to do with economic literature. We hope that this information leads to discussion within the profession of whether this focus is good or bad.

Appendix

Methodology of the Questionnaire

In 1985, 812 doctorates were awarded in economics. Judging from incomplete figures we would estimate that the six schools in our study awarded approximately 110; thus those of our sample schools represent about 14 percent of the total.

The questionnaire was distributed in the spring of 1985. The total number of respondents was 212 from an estimated population of 600–800, an approximate 25–30 percent response rate, normal for this type of study. There were 31 questions and the questionnaire took anywhere from fifteen minutes to more than an hour to fill out. The distribution of respondents by year was roughly equal: first, 24.5 percent; second, 20.8 percent; third, 21.7 percent; fourth, 14.2 percent; and fifth or more, 18.9 percent. We followed up our survey with a series of interviews.

The questionnaires were distributed at the six schools in two ways. Where possible (at all schools except Yale and Columbia), they were placed in individual student mail boxes. At Yale and Columbia they were distributed by a few selected individuals. This accounts for the lower response rate and adds a possible bias in the coverage at those schools. Thus in certain cross-school comparisons we have left those schools out. Determining the total size of the student population is difficult, because schools list individuals who have not finished dissertations as active students even though they may not be active students; still, the response rate was about 40 percent at Harvard, MIT, Chicago, and Stanford. The response rate at Yale and Columbia was lower, but since the results of the survey were not all out of line with the results from the other four schools, it seems reasonable to conclude that the results from these schools are valid.

The potential for bias in these surveys does, however, exist. More technically oriented students may be less likely to answer questionnaires. In our survey there were, for example, relatively few Asian students, who are believed to be more technically oriented than the typical U.S. student. Thus, as with all empirical research, the results must be interpreted with care.

Notes

1. Dropouts are not included in the survey. However, at most of these schools the dropout rate is relatively low. This suggests to us that the admissions process is succeeding in weeding out students who cannot accept the process.

2. The percentages can add up to more than 100 percent because some students choose more than one goal.

3. From top to bottom, Ward's hierarchy was as follows: (1) micro and macro theory, and econometrics; (2) international trade, public finance, and money and banking; (3) labor, industrial organization, and economic history; (4) history of economic theory, economic development, and comparative economic systems.

4. The question was phrased as follows: "Which characteristics will most likely place students on the fast track? Circle one." In our interviews we asked students how they interpreted "fast track" and found that almost all students believed it to refer to success in the academic profession.

5. Perceptions often differ from reality. Robert Solow pointed out to us that he never made such a statement. The likely source for the statement is a quotation from Dale Jorgenson as reported in a *Business Week* article.

4

Workmanship, Incentives, and Cynicism

The survey and the questionnaire discussed in the previous essay effectively show us graduate education in economics at the elite universities. They reveal strengths in graduate economics education. The students are bright, perceptive, and interesting. There's a healthy diversity of the student body, and the programs are demanding and intellectually challenging.

But to the noneconomist observer, the survey and conversations also say that something is wrong with graduate economics education: The enormous division of views between Chicago and the other schools is disturbing. How can people studying a so-called social science have such major differences about the way the economy works? A second finding that will likely trouble the noneconomist is the perception students have that a knowledge of economic literature and economic institutions lacks importance. Is it reasonable for economics educators to place such slight emphasis on literature and institutions? A third concern is the sense of cynicism that came through in many of the written comments and in the conversations. The students knew what would get them ahead; they could do it, but for many the intellectual excitement of science wasn't there.

My views have evolved and themselves been clarified by discussion and significant criticisms of an earlier draft of this essay by Hal Varian and Robert Solow. I suspect we still differ substantially, but their critical comments were helpful in shaping this essay.

The lay reader might be shocked by these findings, but most economists won't be. Our findings were not unexpected. Students feel a lack of reality in what they study because, by design, there is little reality there; the focus on techniques and modeling precludes it. There are such differing views among schools because the views are built into the models and techniques the students learn. Students do not learn—and are not meant to learn—to question or to assess those models. The cynicism is a bit more difficult for economists to be complacent about; graduate schools do not plan to instill cynicism, but cynicism is the natural outcome.

Our survey results will come as no surprise to most mainstream economists. In fact, conscious efforts have been made in the last thirty years to bring about the existing situation. For many economists, therefore, these results are neither shocking nor cause for concern. For them, graduate education is doing what it is supposed to be doing, just as economics is doing what it is supposed to be doing. To say that something is wrong with economics education would be to say that something is wrong with economics, and most mainstream economists don't believe that anything is wrong with economics as it is currently practiced.

To support their view, most mainstream economists point out that economics and graduate economics education are highly successful. Its graduates can get good jobs and in many cases are highly sought after. Economics is making advances in the understanding of the pure theory of markets. It is more unified than any of the other social sciences. In short, it has the outward manifestations of a highly successful discipline.

Thus, contrary to what the layperson might think, to argue that our survey points to something wrong with graduate economics education is to go against the mainstream view. We don't expect to hear this response often: "Oh, look at those results; now let's go out and change the discipline to make it more relevant." But we will hear this: "Oh, it's some more of those superficial Galbraithian critics who don't understand the need for clarity and formalism, taking easy potshots at the profession.''

This chapter tries to justify my criticisms to those in the profession, but its other purpose is to explain to the lay reader the mainstream economics argument and to compare the different views that Klamer, I, and many critics of economics have with the mainstream view.

Let me begin by stating what my criticisms are not. They are not that what economics is doing is irrelevant or that formalism and abstract models are bad. Seeming irrelevance and abstract formalism are a necessary part of any scientific theory. The question is this: Is a focus on formalism enough? Most mainstream economists believe that it is. I do not. I come to a different answer because my view of the methodology of science differs from the view held by most mainstream economists. Because I don't accept the methodological foundations of science that the mainstream accepts, I find myself in the difficult position (and it is difficult for an economist) of agreeing with the layperson. Economics as it is currently practiced and taught is seriously flawed, and because it is flawed, graduate education is flawed.

Methodology and the Survey Results

Because the differing views of the underlying methodological foundations of economics and the role and nature of empirical testing are central to my differences with the mainstream, some discussion of those foundations is needed. Most mainstream economists who are satisfied with the state of economics follow (probably implicitly, because few study methodology) some brand of Popperian or Lakatosian methodology of science, both of which are refinements of logical positivism.[1] A principle of these scientific methodologies is that economics (or any other science) is advanced by the empirical testing of well-specified propositions. According to positivism and its derivatives, that's what science is: one specifies a hypothesis and one tests it. All else is metaphysical sophistry that allows biases and subjectivity to enter the analysis. Good science—good economics—avoids that.

To be well specified, hypotheses must be clearly specified, and if hypotheses are to be clearly specified, students must learn the techniques to specify and test propositions precisely. Teaching students to do that is difficult, but that's the task graduate economics education has set itself. It must teach students how to specify hypotheses clearly and then how to model and test them. In this process, making reasonable assumptions and understanding economic reality in some broad, vague sense are irrelevant. Empirical tests are relied upon to weed out the incorrect theories and extensions of a theory.

In the mainstream methodological view, there's no need for most researchers to have a broad picture of economics research, to know economic literature, or to know economic institutions. Each economist is working on a part of the puzzle—and what I have elsewhere called "the invisible hand of truth" will see to it that the pieces of the puzzle fit together.[2] Yes, the mainstream economists wish the students had a stronger sense of workmanship, but that's a problem in the students; it's not a problem of graduate economics education.

Methodology isn't much talked about in graduate schools, and so the underlying methodology must be deduced from what the graduate schools do and from what they teach. Chicago is unabashedly positivist. For Chicago, the later refinements are unnecessary. The other schools are less positivist, but the nature of what they teach still reflects the positivist outlook.

There is much to be said for the mainstream positivist methodology of science when there is an agreed-upon empirical test for the hypotheses being put forward. But when that consensus is lacking, as it often is in any branch of science, one is left with a wide range of reasonable hypotheses from which one cannot select on the basis of empirical testing. What happens then? A reasonable answer would be that some other selection process should supplement formal empirical testing of hypotheses. But that isn't what happens in economics. The mainstream position is that if it isn't empirically testable by the formal methods, it isn't science.

What is the result? Students are presented with a contradiction. Many, if not most, of the interesting questions in economics are not empirically testable with econometrics. The closest equivalent I can think of is a story I heard about medical school interviews that were designed to reveal if students could handle stress. At the beginning of the interview, the student was asked to open a window. But the window was nailed shut, and when the student could not open it, he or she was berated—and then the interview started.

The human mind is amazing, and it can handle such contradictions. Students resolve the contradictions by (1) doing abstract theoretical work that will be empirically tested at a later date (which often never comes); (2) empirically testing what can't be empirically tested and coming up with results that convince few but are formally impressive; (3) becoming cynical and leaving the economics profession; and (4) developing their own reasonable test criteria and learning on their own.

Telling students to do what can't be done, I argue, characterizes the current state of graduate education in economics. Students are forced to push empirical testing beyond its limits. They do so because they have no choice. If they want their Ph.D.'s, they must empirically test. In reaction, many become cynical and lose their sense of pride in their work. After all, they are presented with a set of tools in their first two years of graduate school and are told to use them in writing a dissertation in their last two years. If they are told to test, they will test as they were taught, whether the tests are appropriate or not.

Clearly, not all economists respond in the same way. Some simply do what can't be done and believe that it can. When professors and peers all say it can be done, some students can convince themselves they are doing it. They test and corroborate their results in an insulated environment, and then when economists at other schools are not convinced by these test, the students attribute the skepticism to bias on the part of the other economists. This approach offers the least dissonance but requires peer support of almost religious fervor. Chicago has excelled at this "solution," and that is why the Chicago students were the happiest with their education. What they were taught to do corresponded with what they were supposed to do.

The other schools, to a greater or lesser extent, see the process of empirical testing as more complicated. They admit this to the students, but don't give them the tools to deal with the more complicated reality. What these students are taught doesn't correspond with what they are supposed to do. The result is the cynicism we detected.

Some people work out alternative methods of choosing among theories, of informally processing nonformal empirical evidence, of integrating institutional knowledge with their formal analysis. As they do so, they become craftspeople, experts in their chosen field of specialty. The results are impressive, and there are a number of mainstream economists whose work is almost universally admired. They have solved this dilemma. They can deal with formalism, informalism, and common sense. I might not always agree with them, but I generally learn something from them and deeply respect their views and ideas. My complaint is that graduate economics programs are not teaching students the craft of economics. The craftspeople in economics learned to do what they do on their own; they weren't taught it in graduate school. And that's what I'm saying is wrong with graduate education. It doesn't give students the tools they need to deal with the economics problems they will face.

I follow a sociological approach to methodology. Unlike the Popperian or Lakatosian methodologies, a sociological approach does not assume that scientists are searching for the truth. Truth is one of their goals but only one; professional advancement, recognition, and wealth are others of perhaps equal or more importance. *Good science is made possible by institutional conventions that make it in scientists' interest to follow reasonable conventions, those most likely to limit subjectivity and bias.* Good science, then, does not come naturally. It comes from limiting, through training, individuals' natural proclivity toward self-interest and instilling in them a yearning passion for the closest approximation to the truth that one can achieve. A sociological approach to methodology is not inconsistent with the mainstream positivist methodology. It is simply broader, and in specific instances it includes the Lakatosian methodology.

A sociological approach to methodology does not deny the importance and persuasiveness of empirical testing if an agreed-upon formal empirical test can be found and replication is possible. In such a case, this formal test guides, and should guide, scientists' action. But the sociological approach accepts that empirical testing is an art and cannot be used as a decision rule for many hypotheses. Positivism says science ends with formal empirical testing; if formal empirical testing is impossible, no science is possible. A sociological approach says that science does not end with formal empirical testing, that there are reasonable ways of processing information upon which people can agree. A sociological approach to methodology expands the domain of science, avoiding, whenever possible, subjective bias.

An economist using a sociological approach will recognize formal empirical testing as itself an agreed-upon convention. It is convincing because people are taught that it is convincing and because it corresponds with their instincts. But it can be biased and subjective, as can all other types of tests. So the issue isn't formal empirical testing versus nonformal empirical testing; the issue is the nature of the appropriate empirical test.

My particular sociological approach to methodology reflects my economic training. It carries economists' assumption of economic rationality to its logical conclusion. Positivism assumes that individuals search for the truth even if it is not in their self-interest. The sociological approach that I use, paradoxically, assumes scientists are the same type of rational beings that neo-classical economics assumes all people are. To be a neo-classical economist whose methodology is positivism is to be inconsistent.

If no agreed-upon convention of processing information exists, self-interest guides choices of theories. When scientific conventions no longer guide scientists' actions, those conventions will be replaced by self-interest and cynicism. That is what I believe has happened in economics. Because the profession has not come to grips with what decision rules to follow when empirical tests are inconclusive, the profession has lost its bearings and has allowed self-interest to govern the choice of theories.[3]

This is the environment in a discipline in which self-interest dominates; models are chosen on the basis of whether they will lead to a publishable article, not on the basis of how illuminating they are. One knows as little literature as possible, because to know literature will force one to attribute ideas to others. Formal empirical tests are not done to answer questions, but to satisfy reviewers and advisors. Pay, not the fulfillment of intellectual curiosity, becomes the scientists' reward.

In an economics discipline guided by self-interest, the sense of joy, of excitement, of trying to explain conundrums in the economy, has been replaced by an intricate game of one-upmanship. For many economists, research is not a way to deepen their understanding of the economy; it's a way of advancing in the profession. The sense of pride and workmanship is gone—replaced with a cynical understanding of how to get ahead.

The students are quick to pick up on the way the profession works. They recognize that the way to advance is to do a model that is slightly different from one of the other models. As one student said, "You never take on some really risky thing . . . the payoff is too low." One doesn't try to relate one's model to reality, to have it add something meaningful to economists' understanding—not because one doesn't want to but because one doesn't have the time. To try to relate one's model to reality means entering into an uncharted area, an area for which one has no training.

Graduate students need only look around to see who the young successful economists are and where the payoffs are. Learn the techniques—or better yet, advance a technique and then figure out a question to ask that can use that technique. The more interesting the question, the better off one is, but if one chooses the questions first and then the technique, one is likely to flounder. As a perceptive Yale student wrote in answer to the question about what leads to success in economics, "Not too critical a mind."

I could present a wide variety of examples to show that economic theories are not testable by generally agreed-upon tests, but I think our survey results as to the differences in views of students at various graduate programs make such a discussion unnecessary. When students can differ as much as do those at Chicago from other students about what theories are correct, there can be no generally accepted empirical test. That doesn't mean that the evidence isn't empirically tested. It's been tested—and not surprisingly, both sides find that they are right, within a 99 percent confidence interval. In turn, I'm 99 percent confident that they aren't both right and that the techniques available don't provide an answer as to which side is right.

In mainstream methodology, therefore, what most economists are doing is not science, which is why they fight so hard against anyone who claims that the propositions aren't formally testable. In sociological methodology, science without definitive formal testing is still possible; one simply must supplement the controlled formal empirical testing with reasoned judgments and sensible interpretations and understanding of all the available empirical evidence. The formal empirical tests must be supplemented by informal tests, making a wider range of empirical observations play a role in deciding among theories.

Models have a much different role in sociological methodology than they do in positivist methodology. In positivist methodology, models are ways of deriving formal testable hypotheses. To do so, they must be extraordinarily precise and clear so that they will yield formally testable hypotheses. In sociological methodology, models serve an organizing role. They structure one's thinking about a problem and make it possible to consider the problem in an orderly fashion. To serve this purpose, they do not have to be precise; in fact, precision can destroy the purpose of the model by diverting one's focus from the general ideas to the technical aspects of the model—by making it more difficult to keep in the back of one's mind the applicability of the model.

If this sociological methodology were adopted, economics would be more meaningful, and graduate economics students would be less cynical.

What to Do about the Current State of Affairs

The economics profession must establish a set of conventions to guide students so they can deal effectively with a wider range of empirical evidence—so they can learn to make reasoned, and reasonable, judgments that employ the available empirical evidence. Unless something is done, self-interest will guide economists' work. There is no invisible hand that guides economists to search for the truth; scientific conventions established over long periods work as an invisible hand, but these conventions themselves must be guided. What is needed in economics is the establishment of a set of conventions that can guide scientific inquiry when formal empirical testing cannot.[4]

Establishing Nonformalist Conventions

Establishing nonformal empirical, or sociological, conventions is much more difficult than establishing formal empirical conventions because the appropriate nonformal empirical conventions are quite different from, and even contradict, good formal empirical conventions. For example:

• The positivist convention is that there is no reason to know institutions; in fact, it can be harmful because too much institutional information can cause one to lose sight of the forest for the trees. Assumptions must be unrealistic. The sociological convention is that to talk reasonably about an institution, one must know it intimately; if one is to judge a model, one must know why the model's assumptions differ from reality and why making those assumptions does not do an injustice to the model.

• The positivist convention is that the latest literature embodies all that is worth knowing from earlier literature. To know economic literature is nice, but it is not part of formal scientific discovery. The sociological convention is that one must know the past literature of one's field. Only then can one know the variety of viewpoints and choose the viewpoint most appropriate for the problem at hand.

• The positivist convention is that one should know only the paradigm within which one works. Formal empirical testing will decide among competing theories. The sociological convention is that one must know all paradigms so that one can use common sense in choosing which approach sheds most light on a particular issue.

I could go on, but I think the point is made. Integrating good sociological conventions with positivist conventions will not be easy; it requires split personalities. On the one hand, one must maintain a narrow, scientific specialization; on the other hand, one must maintain a humanistic breadth. A good economist must do both simultaneously.

How Did Economics Evolve into Its Current State?

There has been a continual pull in economics between the positivist scientific conventions and the broader sociological conventions. Thus, to understand the current situation in economics, one must understand its history. Adam Smith was sociological; David Ricardo was formalist. The German historical school was sociological; Leon Walras was formalist. Alfred Marshall was sociological; Paul Samuelson is formalist. The ongoing history of economics is one of a swing between the two approaches.

In the early 1930s in the United States, the sociological approach dominated. Students learned economic literature and institutions. In the late 1930s, John Hicks and Paul Samuelson demonstrated the power of formal positivism and started economics along its present path. They showed that many of the previous economic views were biased and confused, and they added clarity to a wide range of economic propositions. Yet the sociological conventions still lingered, and students in the 1940s and 1950s received training in both traditions. By the late 1960s, the formalists dominated the profession, and today this domination is almost complete.

An important reason for their domination was the development of econometrics. In the 1960s and 1970s, with the progress of computers, the possibilities of formal empirical testing expanded enormously. Econometrics developed as a way of formally testing hypotheses and added another skill for economists to master. The curriculum was squeezed, and slowly the teaching of sociological conventions was pushed out. History of economic thought was eliminated as a requirement; economic history was eliminated; the teaching of any institutional material was eliminated; and the teaching of reasoned judgment was eliminated as being potentially biased. Students in the 1960s still received some of this training (their professors were from that tradition), but the upcoming, younger economists increasingly had less. The emphasis shifted to technical skills. Applied economics came to mean less and less familiarity with the institutions in an area or field and more and more knowledge of how to work with data sets.

In the 1950s and 1960s, this change was not seen as a loss; it was believed that econometrics would offer economics a formal empirical test that could rid it of many of the subjective biases inherent in nonformal argumentation. Consistent with that belief, economic literature and economic institutions were purged from the graduate economics curriculum and replaced with the teaching of techniques that would better allow economists to set up testable hypotheses and with econometrics that would better allow economists to test their theories. Unfortunately, the development of high-speed computers worked counter to, rather than in support of, making economics reflect the real world.

When foundations gave universities grants to set up ''applied'' seminars and to encourage students to do ''applied'' work, ''applied'' work no longer meant real-world work. ''Applied'' quickly came to mean ''also trained in econometrics,'' and it added another technical specialty that economists were expected to have.

High-speed computers did not make economics more applied. Although they improved economists' technical ability to test theories, they reduced economists' ability to judge the appropriateness of their theories. Before the existence of high-speed computers, economists had to dirty their hands when they did applied economics. They had to work through the data—organizing it, sometimes even collecting it—but generally dirtying their hands. It was slow, tedious work, but it had a by-product: It gave economists who did it a sense of the data, the problems with the data, and the institutions they were studying. They knew the institutions—they had to in order to get their data.

Today, self-collection of data is rare. Instead, an economist gets a computer tape of some panel data and tests using the information on that tape. This is an extremely efficient way to handle large amounts of data, but it involves an enormous loss of interpretive information. What's missing are the comments, the sensibility of the survey collector, the knowledge of whether the person answered truthfully or not, or how robust the data are. Some economists have that sense, and when one hears their arguments, they are convincing. But the majority do not fill in the gaps; they rely on the information as fed to them by the tapes, and thus they no longer have a sense of the real-world institutions they are studying.

In short, unless economists train themselves, they get little feel for the way the world works. Instead, they learn the way their model of the world works and how knowledge of that model will advance them in their profession.

Graduate and Undergraduate Economics Training

Some mainstream economists with whom I have discussed this issue agree that there is a problem with economics education, but they argue that the problem lies in undergraduate, not graduate, education. Although they lament the focus on technique in graduate education, they claim they must bring the students up to speed because undergraduate education has not done its job.

They point out that undergraduate natural science majors learn the techniques. Why can't undergraduate economics majors do the same? These arguments have some merit, especially for those who still follow a positivist methodology, but the changes they call for are not possible, given the institutional structure of U.S. education. To see why, we must consider the relationship between graduate and undergraduate education.

Economics is in a position different from the natural sciences. Because most undergraduate natural science departments can assume that at least a sizable minority of their majors plan to pursue science careers, they can structure the program to prepare students for graduate school. Economics departments cannot take this approach. Most undergraduate economics students have no intention of becoming scientists. They're going into business and have a consumer's interest in economics, not a producer's interest. The reality is that most students who major in economics are actually business majors in disguise. At schools where there is a business program, the number of economics majors drops dramatically. Liberal arts schools, where most economics majors are enrolled, would be doing a serious disservice to the majority of their majors if they taught a curriculum that would bring students up to speed in techniques used in graduate school. Not only would they be doing a serious disservice, they would lose, probably, 90–95 percent of their economics majors.

Put bluntly, the large demand for economics professors exists because of economics' relationship to business. Were undergraduate schools to make economics a true pre–graduate-school preparation, the demand for economists to teach in these undergraduate schools would decline significantly—so much so that many of the new Ph.D.'s in economics would be unable to find jobs. Teaching economics is what most Ph.D. economists do.

The same pressures to teach real-world economics are felt in economics programs at schools where there are business departments. The demand for their services comes from servicing business school students, and if they are to get majors, they must keep the level of technique they teach far below that of graduate schools.

This does not mean that undergraduate economics programs don't use mathematical techniques. Many use techniques as a way of regulating the number of majors. If there is a shortage of majors, lower techniques; if there is a surplus of majors (depending on the political relationship the department has with the dean), raise techniques. But we're talking quantum levels below the techniques used in graduate schools.

Undergraduate economics training could focus on economic literature and institutions and on reasonably interpreting nonformal empirical data. This approach would be useful for business students and would make undergraduate economics an integral part of an economics education. But who is to teach these courses? Outgoing graduate students have a strong desire to teach what they've learned in graduate school, and at present they are ill prepared to teach in such a program. Instead, these new teachers initially design undergraduate programs to mimic graduate programs. It is only when they are faced with the reality of teaching students who are completely indifferent to what the teachers are doing that they acquire, through on-the-job training, a knowledge of economic institutions sufficient to get by in the classroom. But it's no thanks to their graduate training. Graduate economics students receive little useful training for teaching undergraduates.

Many top liberal arts schools that I know lament what is going on in graduate schools. What the graduate schools are teaching their students is not especially useful for what their students will be required to teach when they take up classroom teaching themselves. We hire their graduates because the graduate schools have a monopoly (the top schools call themselves ''the cartel'') and because they get the brightest students. We hire from the best graduate schools because they serve as a screening device, not because of what they teach their students.

Providing undergraduate education is the largest job that the economics profession does. Graduate programs in economics depend upon the demand for undergraduate economics courses to justify their budgets to university administrators. They supply the graduate students to teach the courses (at bargain wages) and once in a while supply upper-level professors to teach an undergraduate course. For many graduate programs, a shortfall of graduate students will bring the dean upon their heads, not because of what it means for the graduate program but for what it means for the undergraduate program. Covering the undergraduate program is how the graduate programs "earn their keep." Graduate students are the input that keeps the undergraduate program going—and thereby keeps the graduate departments going.

Thus, at each level, there is a need to rely on the demand from undergraduate students interested in business to maintain the current demand for economists. Were the undergraduate economics curriculum designed to prepare students for what they are taught in graduate economics, graduate programs would have to shrink by at least 50 percent. My suspicion is that faced with this reality, most economists would not choose the shrinkage option. Another option—running separate tracks for pre-graduate school majors and students who aren't going on to graduate school—isn't actually an option for most schools because the number of potential candidates for graduate school is so small that the administration can't justify a program designed only for them. So undergraduate economics education will remain what it is: a general introduction to economics—a mix of lowbrow theory, institutional knowledge, and economic reasoning—because that is what the demand is for. And so most undergraduate economics majors will remain ill-prepared for graduate school.

This state of affairs brings about two reactions. The first reaction is that graduate programs know that undergraduate programs are not preparing students for graduate school and don't require their entrants to have studied economics. Although an undergraduate major is almost essential for graduate studies in fields such as chemistry, physics, and engineering, it is not necessary in economics. Graduate schools accept many students who have no background in economics, and while it is somewhat of a limitation for the students, in our survey it is apparent that for graduate students in economics a mathematics background was a better background than an economics undergraduate background. In fact, I'm told that individuals who can't get a Ph.D. in math are directed to apply to economics, where they not only can get a Ph.D. but can be stars.

The second reaction is that the word goes out as to what is required in graduate schools, and undergraduate majors with good interpretive skills shy away from graduate economics programs. They hear from their undergraduate advisors that unless they are willing to go through training that will seem to them like jumping through hoops, they should not go to graduate school in economics. The only students who apply are those who think they can put up with—or who actually enjoy—jumping through hoops; many of the brightest students with excellent interpretive skills drop out. As a number of students told us when they commented on our survey results: "If you think the responses you got were of concern, you should talk to so-and-so, who dropped out." The selection process is screening out those individuals with the interpretive skills to deal effectively with nonformal empirical evidence. Students who go into and get through graduate economics programs are those who will accept technical modeling for its own sake. And these will become the next generation of teachers.

So the institutional situation is as follows: Undergraduate economics programs are, of necessity, general nontechnical programs; it is left to graduate programs to teach both the technique and the sensibility. Graduate programs teach technique, leaving students to learn interpretive skills and sensibility on their own. Most don't; they become undergraduate teachers, and institutional content and interpretive skills are given an even lower ranking in the next generation.

There is no easy way out of the current state of economics. It is a self-reinforcing state that will require Herculean efforts to change, because change goes against the very interests of the individuals who would be required to make that change. Unfortunately, history provides few examples of such changes from within. Instead, institutions go through the motions of implementing change, but they do not change. That seems to be the path chosen by the economics profession.

In response to our survey, the American Economics Association established a commission (made up primarily of graduate-level economics professors) to study graduate education. Spending hundreds of thousands of dollars, they conducted surveys of large numbers of groups to see if major changes were necessary. I have not seen the survey, let alone its results, but I will make a nonformal empirical prediction about the findings: those results will be that there is some reason for concern about the nature of graduate economics education but it is fundamentally sound. It is doing what it is intended to do, and what it should do, subject to minor changes. Perhaps, if my empirical prediction is correct, some positivist economists who choose theories on the basis of predictability might take seriously the need for change.

Notes

1. I present a more extended discussion of methodology in Harry Landreth and David Colander, *History of Economic Theory*, 2d ed. (Boston: Houghton Mifflin, 1989).

2. The "invisible hand of truth" is found in a paper of that title in *The Spread of Economic Ideas*, ed. Colander and Coats (Boston: Cambridge University Press, 1989), reprinted in this volume, pp. 81–88.

3. In "The Evolution of Keynesian Economics," I treat the evolution of macroeconomics, arguing that economists' self-interest, more than politics or empirical findings, has guided the evolution of macroeconomic theories. "The Evolution of Keynesian Economics," in *Keynes and Public Policy*, ed. Omar Hamouda and John Smithen (Aldershot, England: Edward Elgar, 1988), reprinted in this volume, pp. 91–101.

4. To some degree, the development of Baysian econometrics is moving in the direction of establishing an alternative, more believable, formal empirical test, but it is still in its infancy and, most likely, will simply present econometric tests in a more honest fashion rather than expand the domain of empirical testing.

5

The Invisible Hand of Truth

In a biting critique of the economics profession, Robert Clower (1989) suggests that much of the profession is irrelevant, more concerned with techniques and game playing than with ideas. Because it is irrelevant, many economists do not take their own subject seriously. He asks, "How many footnotes do we need?" In my view, Clower's critique of the profession is correct; the spread of economic ideas is seriously undermined by the educational institutions that have developed in the United States.

Arguing that much of what economists do is irrelevant goes against what is currently in vogue in the philosophy of science; most scientists seem implicitly to believe that there exists an invisible hand which guides science to the truth. In this normal science view, scientists search after understanding by dividing up a set of questions and trying to answer one small subset of those questions. Their answer to the question: "Does this lead to Truth?" is, "Yes, each researcher is looking at only a small part of the puzzle, but, combined, economists' research is the best way of approaching truth." As Solow (1989) argues, this normal science view is the generally held view of what economists do within the profession. Yes, he agrees, there are some minor problems; some researchers are doing irrelevant work, but these are problems of any scientific profession; in total, economics is not that bad and no worse than any other field.

The view that Clower, I, and many other critics of the profession hold is that in economics normal science has run amok. The invisible hand of truth has lost its guiding influence. Clearly, some normal science, and some advancement in understanding, takes place, but that advancement is the exception, not the rule, and may not even be large enough to replace what is forgotten. The reason why economics has run amok is to be found in the sociological approach to economics which focuses on the internal dynamics of the profession: who is allowed to become a member, who gets promoted, who gets paid what, who gets the laurels, as opposed to the external dynamics which consider how truth-seeking individuals can best find truth. Philosophers of science have given short shrift to the internal dynamics (which they see as external to science); they assume that researchers have a desire to find the truth and do their best to answer questions that will advance science. They believe that if they can specify a scientific method that will most likely lead to discovering the truth, then researchers will follow that scientific method. But that is simply an assumption. They do not logically show why people want to discover the truth.

The sociological approach to methodology that I follow is more agnostic; it allows that people may have an inherent desire to discover the truth, but they may not, either because they aren't interested or because the internal dynamics in the profession direct self-interest toward other ends. There is a connection between self-interest and discovering the truth—the individual who advances knowledge advances in the profession—but it is a loose and often tenuous connection, and frequently the two diverge. The reasons they diverge are numerous: the requirements for advancing understanding change quickly, while the institutions within which that search for knowledge takes place change only slowly. Deriving the financial support for research requires different skills than does actually doing research, and there is a difficulty of deciding what advancement is.

Combined, these leave most academic disciplines in a quandary. Some, like English literary criticism, make no pretense of advancement. They simply try to maintain a steady state of knowledge. Others, such as sociology or political science or anthropology, become fragmented, and each group does its own thing, with little agreement about what is advancement. Economics is amazingly coherent compared to the other social sciences. It has a "grand theory" accepted by a large majority of the profession, and an accepted methodology. However, that coherence does not come from a well-defined set of questions which researchers are trying to answer; rather, it comes from a core of knowledge that almost all economists believe should be mastered by an economist. That core knowledge is embodied in the core curriculum of graduate school economics programs and consists of a set of techniques and problem-solving algorithms. Economics is tied together not by a common set of questions, but a common set of techniques.

The lack of a well-defined set of questions which, if answered, everyone agrees would advance understanding, is in part explained by the difficulty in empirical testing. Other formerly considered hard sciences—for example, modern physics—are becoming more conjectural as the costs of empirically testing various theories become more forbidding.

Such a state of affairs is most conducive to internal, rather than external, dynamics guiding the profession. In the absence of an agreed-upon specific set of questions researchers are attempting to answer, most research is done and most papers are written to establish positions for internal reasons. Economics research has become more a move in a game of chess than a search for understanding reality. An example is the recent spread of rational expectations in macroeconomics.

Rational expectations is a neat idea and makes the analysis of expectations an integral part of economic analysis. Early on, it was apparent to many, if not most, economic researchers that there were limitations on rational expectations as applied to macroeconomics. These included multiple equilibria making the delineation of a unique rational expectation impossible; informational problems; and game-theoretic problems. These difficulties, which most economists now agree make the rational expectations hypothesis untestable, did not stop economists from developing large numbers of rational expectations macro models which differed from one another by an assumption here or there. The result was the New Classical Revolution. Younger Keynesians quickly got in on the game; finance-constrained rational expectations models soon appeared which provided a theoretical justification for Keynesian policies even assuming rational expectations. By developing these models, graduate students and professors demonstrated that they could jump through hoops; the more hoops they could jump through the higher their income, chances for promotion, and standing in the profession. For many economists economic research has become the art of devising clever models and in doing so demonstrating one's technical virtuosity.

Rational expectations is only one example. There are many others. Econometric work often is done to demonstrate mastery of new techniques rather than to answer questions. General equilibrium models with an infinite number of traders, optimal taxation models, screening models—all fit the same mold. Empirically they are difficult, if not impossible, to test. Impossibility of empirical testing does not, and should not, stop economists from writing about a subject. But it does change the optimal form that the writing should take. If an idea can't be tested, it should be conveyed in as understandable a way as possible because ultimately others will judge it by the commonsense test. Does it make intuitive sense? Is it reasonable? The formal models that fill the economics journals are difficult to judge by the commonsense test or can't be judged by that test at all. But nonetheless they are conceived and published. The reason is simple. The incentives in the economics profession are for articles, not ideas.

To remain an academic economist one must get tenure. Getting tenure means getting published. Economists who follow the academic route must publish their ideas in the form of articles, preferably in the best journals. Books, for some reason, count for little in the academic economics profession; books that are readable by the lay public count for less than nothing and can be the cause of an otherwise qualified person's not getting tenure. John Kenneth Galbraith, who stopped writing for the profession and began writing directly to the public relatively early in his career, has stated that if he were advising a young economist today, he would advise that economist to write highly mathematical articles and not follow the route he himself took.

To say that the incentives within the system are for articles, not ideas, is not to say that the profession does not value ideas. If most economists were asked, they would respond that it is good ideas and insights, not articles, that should get a person tenure. However, because ideas cannot be quantitatively measured, and articles can, schools generally rely on articles as a proxy for good ideas. And when one is up for tenure, any article that can get published is a good idea.

If there were a relatively close correlation between ideas and articles, this proxy would be acceptable, but there is not. Generally, the easiest impressive-looking articles to write do not involve exploring new ideas or ideas useful in policy; they involve using a new technique or formalizing a simple idea that is well known. Thus, that type of article predominates. Differentiating nonformal articles that say something from those that do not is exceptionally difficult. Thus, to write a good nonformalist article that will be perceived as being good is risky, if not downright crazy, especially when the individuals deciding what is good take a formalist approach.

The incentive system is readily ferreted out by economists. In a study Arjo Klamer and I did of graduate economics education (page 47), we asked students what would put them on the fast track. Approximately 90 percent said that knowledge of mathematics and knowledge of modeling were important; only about 3 percent said that these were unimportant. Only 10 percent said that knowledge of economic literature was very important and only 3 percent said that knowledge of the economy was very important. Sixty-eight percent said knowledge of the economy was unimportant (Colander and Klamer 1987). In my view, these answers suggest that something is terribly wrong in the economics profession and in the incentives that economists perceive.

No one is saying that, where possible, a formal model is not preferred to an informal model. But when mind-sets become so fixated on formal models that individuals cannot deal with ideas outside of these models, then it is not surprising that many believe that economics has lost its bearings.

An example of the problem is the way in which economists deal with institutions. Put simply, in many of their models they assume them away, not because they believe institutions are unimportant but because institutions cannot be neatly modeled. The needs of formalist expression overwhelm the needs of common sense, and clarity of the models gets in the way of clarity of meaning.

At dinner one night I described a proposal that I had written to an economist—a graduate of a top graduate program. After listening to my account of the proposal, he asked if I had a formal model for it. When I said no, he said that he didn't believe, and could not even think about, a proposal that wasn't formally modeled. Now, I am not saying that the idea was good or bad; what I am saying is that informally expressed ideas should be able to get a hearing within the economics profession. Generally, they cannot.

If the experience described above were unique, it could be dismissed. But it is the rule, not the exception. The majority of young economists today either will not, or cannot, deal with ideas not presented in formal models. In their pursuit of logical, rigorous models, they have lost their common sense.

Creating the current economics mind-set does not come easy, and the molding of students starts early. Most undergraduate economics courses are courses in models and modeling (although the models use much easier math than those in graduate economic courses). Much of the institutional richness which characterizes applied economics is removed from the analysis. Anyone who cannot accept modeling for the sake of modeling drops out. The few nonconformists who somehow nonetheless continue their study of economics into graduate school are usually weeded out in the first year.

In a perverse sort of way, the focus on modeling for the sake of modeling nicely serves the interest of the profession. Strong incentives toward modeling exist in both the suppliers and demanders of economic ideas conveyed in textbooks. Consider, first, the students' incentives. Students' immediate interest is to get good grades, or at least to pass. If they learn too, that's nice, but for most students, their immediate concern is grades. In many ways, they prefer neat models because such models offer a closer correlation between study and grades than do less formal methods of conveying information. When one learns models, if one studies, one can assure oneself of an A. Studying ideas is necessarily vague and will likely lead to a wider variation in grades. Then, as modeling gets built into the courses, students who don't like modeling don't stay in economics. Faculty also have an incentive toward modeling. Teaching models is much easier than teaching ideas. It takes less time to prepare and less thought. Thus, models meet both students' and faculties' needs.

For both of these reasons, ideas that work their way into textbooks are often skewed to what is teachable and graphical rather than to what makes the most sense in some larger context. I would go even further and suggest that unless an idea can be reduced to a simple graph, it has almost no chance of entering the core of what is taught in economics at the undergraduate level.

It is not simply the incentives within the economics profession that are perverse, it is also the incentives within the entire academic community. For example, almost all ideas have political and social, as well as economic, components, but the fragmentation of social science disciplines, like restrictive work practices, limits how those ideas can be passed on.

The above arguments have been suggestive rather than conclusive. They have, I hope, been sufficiently suggestive to provide a prima facie case that internal incentives within the profession should make one question whether the invisible hand guiding economics toward the truth is not, instead, an invisible foot stomping on anyone with the audacity to scream that the emperor has no clothes.

An Addendum

The above discussion has been critical of the economics profession, and I want to end on a more positive note, so that I will not be misinterpreted. All real-world systems involve perverse incentives. The perverse incentives in any real-world system must be judged in relation to the incentives in other real-world systems, not those in ideal systems. I am not making the argument that economics is uniquely perverse. Much in the world is perverse. Thus, when considering alternative institutions, it is important not to condemn a system automatically because it exhibits perverse incentives. My argument is simply that the system deserves to be considered more carefully than it has been. How we should change economic institutions is a complex question of comparative institutional analysis. It is, however, a question that should be addressed.

3

Applications to
Macroeconomics

6

The Evolution of Keynesian Economics: From Keynesian to New Classical to New Keynesian

To have been born as an economist before 1936 was a boon—yes. But not to have been born too long before!

Bliss was it in that dawn to be alive,
But to be young was very heaven!
[William Wordsworth, *The Prelude*, 1805]

The *General Theory* caught most economists under the age of thirty-five with the unexpected virulence of a disease first attacking and decimating an isolated tribe of South Sea Islanders. Economists beyond fifty turned out to be quite immune to the ailment.
(Paul Samuelson, *"The General Theory* in 1936," 1964)

Paul Samuelson's reflection on the Keynesian revolution captures the excitement that young economists felt about Keynesian economics in the 1930s; it captures the enormous creative development in macroeconomics and Keynesian economic thinking that occurred in the period from 1936 to the mid-1960s. During this period Keynesian macroeconomics moved from being a radical idea of a few young Turks to being the mainstream view of the profession.

In the mid-1960s the theoretical Keynesian revolution began sputtering, and by the mid-1970s it came to a complete halt;

Keynesians under thirty-five became the endangered species; only those economists over fifty remained Keynesians, and many of them went into the closet. The 1970s disease which infected the under-thirty-five economists was New Classical economics, and by the early 1980s the press had declared Keynesian economics dead and New Classical economics the mainstream macroeconomic view.

New Classical economics did not remain mainstream for long. By the mid-1980s New Classical economics was itself on the verge of being wiped out by a new strain of Keynesianism, New Keynesian economics, which was immune to the New Classical virus. This chapter recounts this evolution, considering the questions: Why did the evolution occur as it did? What is the future evolution of macroeconomic theory likely to be?

For those who don't follow closely the theoretical debates in macroeconomics, the labels New Classical and New Keynesian probably have little meaning, so, first, I shall briefly describe what I mean by them.[1] In the mid-1970s New Classicals replaced monetarists as the main opposition to Keynesians. Whereas monetarism is a semiformal analysis, New Classical economics is highly formal. Its analysis blends in assumptions of rational expectations and market clearing within a general equilibrium framework. It initially was called "rational expectations" theory, but as it became apparent that the other elements were necessary to its analysis and policy conclusions, the nomenclature changed from rational expectations theory to New Classical theory. Leading New Classical economists include Robert Barro, Robert Lucas, Thomas Sargent, and Neil Wallace.

The rise of New Keynesian economics is, in part, responsible for the change in nomenclature. New Keynesian theory uses the same formal general equilibrium methodological framework as New Classical theory uses, but it does not use the market clearing assumption. A New Keynesian article looks similar in form to a New Classical article, but because it does not assume market clearing, the conclusion New Keynesians come to is that there is a potential role for government policy. New Keynesians see individual decisions leading to macro externalities, so that individual decisions do not necessarily lead to socially optimal results. The policy question New Keynesians ask is how to internalize the macroeconomic externality.

Their research program includes consideration of such issues as implicit contracts and price signaling problems which provide justification for their nonmarket clearing assumption. Some leading New Keynesians include John Taylor, Joseph Stiglitz, George Akerlof, Greg Mankiw, and Peter Howitt.

In considering the evolution of macroeconomic thinking most commentators have focused on what I call the external approach to paradigm shifts: how well paradigms have accorded with reality and how well the theories predict (or predicted). While not denying the importance of external criteria, given the nature of empirical proof in economics and the need for data interpretation, many theories can accord with reality. To choose among the set of acceptable theories (a set which is, in my view, quite large) another explanation is necessary.

The additional explanation that I want to focus on is what I call the internal approach to paradigm shifts. This internal approach, in my view, plays a key role in the evolution of macroeconomic thinking.[2] The internal approach is quite simple: It suggests that researchers' needs and incentives determine which theory researchers use. For economists, two needs stand out.[3] The first, which I call the article criterion, is a need to publish. To succeed, graduate students need topics upon which to write "good" dissertations and professors need topics about which to write. These topics must be simple enough to be "doable" but sufficiently difficult to impress advisors and reviewers. The more article and dissertation topics that can be extracted from a theory, the better it meets the article criterion.

A paradigm which is article-laden is contagious; it will generate enormous interest and will spread quickly among the profession. However, over time the contagiousness of a paradigm will diminish as the earliest researchers use the richest topics (easy topics which seem hard), leaving later researchers with an increasingly difficult task. Without internal evolution which generates new doable articles and dissertations, over time a theory will become sterile and will no longer be the subject of research.

Whether a theory will have a lasting effect depends on a second internal need. To have a lasting effect a theory must be teachable. The teachability criterion follows from the organization of economic research. In addition to publishing, most economists interested in theory must teach. Given current U.S. teaching institutions, teachability means that the theory must be reducible to a simple model that captures its essence and can be conveyed to students at beginning and intermediate levels.[4] Only theories that are teachable will be integrated into textbooks. Once a theory is integrated in the textbooks, it will continue to have influence and will form the basic understanding of the majority of students and lay public.

The Keynesian theory (1930s-style) fulfilled these internal criteria superbly; it provided numerous dissertation and article topics, as can be seen by the outpouring of simple models which filled the journals in the late 1940s and early 1950s. In these early years, the simultaneous development of national income accounts and econometrics led to an enormous number of empirical questions the new theory could explore and answer.

Through the mid-1960s the evolution of macro models was sufficiently fast to offset the diminishing returns in article production, keeping articles relatively easy to come by for new researchers. Articles continued to flow from the models relatively easily as the simple consumption function model of the 1950s evolved into the neo-Keynesian IS/LM (Investment = Savings/ Liquidity = Money)-aggregate supply/aggregate demand models of the 1960s and 1970s. But it was becoming more and more difficult.

Keynesian and neo-Keynesian economics also nicely met the teachability criterion. It was eminently reducible to simple neat models, as is demonstrated by the rapid acceptance of Lorie Tarshis's and Paul Samuelson's texts, which provided simple models of Keynesian thinking. Even today, after Keynesian models have been discarded on the high theoretical level, they form the basis of what is taught at the beginning and intermediate levels of macroeconomics.

As the Keynesian revolution progressed, it diverged from a less well-publicized revolution in economics, the general equilibrium revolution. This revolution also began in the 1930s, as research shifted away from a Marshallian partial equilibrium framework toward a Walrasian general equilibrium framework. This general equilibrium paradigm offered a variety of research topics, although they were on a recognizably higher level of difficulty than Keynesian research topics and required more technical skills to undertake. Thus fewer researchers considered it, but those who did found publication easy. Because it was difficult, economists working in the area acquired respect. However, in part because of its complicated nature, general equilibrium theory did not meet the teachability criterion. It was difficult to translate its ideas into a simple model that could be taught at the undergraduate level. Thus the general equilibrium revolution remained a theoretical revolution and never significantly affected textbook economics. What is still taught at the beginning and intermediate levels of economics is largely grounded in Marshallian economics, while what is done on the higher level is generally Walrasian.[5]

In the 1950s the Keynesian revolution advanced independently of the general equilibrium revolution with only minimal interaction. But in the 1960s macroeconomics was losing its researchers to microeconomics and to the more technically impressive general equilibrium models. By this time mathematical techniques used in economics had progressed to the point that work on algebraic Keynesian models, even relatively large ones solved by determinants, no longer was sufficiently impressive to generate dissertation topics or articles.

The decline of Keynesian economics was exacerbated by a compromise between neo-Keynesians and neo-Classicals.[6] This compromise based the difference between neo-Keynesians and neo-Classicals on the fixed-wage assumption of neo-Keynesians.

The neo-Keynesian models were awarded the practical laurels; while the neo-Classicals, basing their models on some version of price flexibility caused by the admittedly unrealistic real balance effect, were awarded the theoretical laurels.

While many Keynesians believe that the fixed-wage neo-Keynesian model did not capture the true problem that Keynes had identified, the Classical-Keynesian debates simply died, in large part because of internal criteria. Neither the Keynesian research program nor the alternative monetarist research program (which was making the Classical case) was appropriate to use the new mathematical techniques which were developing during this time. In fact, if anything, monetarists used less sophisticated techniques than did Keynesians. Thus, even though the debate was still relevant and the issues were unresolved, it was dropped.

Rather than work on extending the neo-Keynesian model, theoretically inclined economists and graduate students worked on incorporating macroeconomic models with general equilibrium models and on finding microfoundations for macroeconomics. This work had little or no relation to neo-Keynesian models.[7] The mid-1960s brought about a burgeoning literature in two areas: (1) microfoundations as exemplified by Edmund Phelps's book (1970), which considered the theoretical foundations of the Phillips curve; and (2) translating Keynesian models into general disequilibrium models, exemplified by the work of economists such as Robert Barro and H. Grossman, and E. Malinvaud.

Combined, these two literatures undermined the Keynesian hold on macroeconomic theory. The general equilibrium models cemented the need for fixed nominal wages as the key to the Keynesian conclusion. Within the context of Barro and Grossman's general disequilibrium model that assumption was crucial. The microfoundations work provided alternative explanations of underemployment based on search models. Such models offered far more dissertation topics and articles than did the Keynesian model. Thus by the late 1960s the neo-Keynesian model was doomed.

Real-world events in the 1970s finished the job and allowed

the new work to gather momentum; inflation undermined all but the teaching purpose of the neo-Keynesian model. Here was the open wound that allowed New Classical economics, which emerged from the microfoundations work, to enter.

The evolution away from Keynesian economics began before there were significant empirical problems with the Keynesian model, suggesting that that evolution was primarily fueled by internal rather than external criteria. Were the movement not directed by internal criteria, rather than fueling New Classical economics the inflation could have provided an opening for a resurgence of monetarism since New Classical policy conclusions differed little from monetarist ones.[8]

New Classical economics emerged from the theoretical work in the 1960s by an interesting chain of events. The microfoundations work provided an intuitive story of unemployment. At the same time, the Keynesian story of unemployment caused by fixed wages which emerged from the neo-Keynesian model was undermined by adding rational expectations to the model. New Classicals showed that by adding the idea of rational expectations, assuming long-run wage flexibility but not short-run wage flexibility in a competitive model did not make theoretical sense. As long as there are no constraints on an individual's action (and the formal neo-Keynesian competitive model had none), anything that will happen in the long run will also happen in the short run, as long as people have rational expectations. Using variations of this simple argument, New Classicals argued that to assume fixed nominal wages, without explaining why wages were fixed, was unacceptable.

The argument convinced Barro, one of the two Keynesian researchers who had developed the general disequilibrium Keynesian model. His conversion played an important role in the New Classical revolution and brought about a major change in macroeconomics. Economic journalists figured that if this bright former Keynesian believed it, there must be something in it. Thus he became a leading New Classical theorist and wrote the first New Classical textbook (Barro 1984).

The New Classical revolution initially met the article criterion nicely and thereby spread fast. It also died relatively fast because of internal criteria. Its use of high-level mathematical and econometric techniques contributed to its early success, but those same high-level mathematical and econometric techniques were also damaging to its longevity. Quickly the New Classical modeling was carried to such heights that it was beyond the range of almost all graduate students and economists. Combined with the fact that the empirical results flowing from New Classical economics were both difficult to interpret and inconclusive, New Classical economics soon exhausted the good dissertation topics.

The New Classical theory also failed on the teachability criterion. While there was a nice metaphor to describe the New Classical idea, there was no simple model which could be taught and built into the textbook. Barro's book attempted to codify New Classical economics, but the result was a macroeconomic textbook which, if taught generally, would reduce the number of intermediate macro courses across the country by at least 50 percent. Because it lacked a textbook model, New Classical economics was destined for a blaze of glory that would forever change the theoretical macroeconomics terrain but could not become mainstream macroeconomics. All successful macroeconomic textbooks except Barro's are organized around an IS/LM framework, and there seems little chance of change in the near future.[9]

New Classical economics did, however, make a difference. It shocked Keynesians out of their complacent acceptance of the fixed-wage neo-Keynesian model and provoked a new consideration of the underpinnings of alternative Keynesian models, written in the style of New Classical models and including rational expectations, but which came to Keynesian conclusions. This work is what I call "New Keynesian." New Classical economics also provoked a reconsideration of the historical foundations of Keynesian economics. Finally, it led to a modification of neo-Keynesian models, so they are less dependent on assumptions of wage inflexibility. Combined, this work suggests that Keynesian economics is making a comeback and some version of it is likely to be the mainstream through the 1990s.

Empirical evidence that Keynesian economics lives can be seen in survey results by Frey et al. (1984) and Colander and Klamer (1987). In both these surveys only about 10 percent of the economists surveyed believed fiscal policy was not an effective policy (a New Classical would take the position that fiscal policy is totally ineffective), and only 17 percent of all graduate students saw the rational expectations assumption (a key element in New Classical economics) as very important. Forty percent saw the New Keynesian assumption of imperfect competition as very important, and only 10 percent saw it as unimportant.

Given the variety of Keynesian responses to New Classical economics, the current state of Keynesian macroeconomics is one of confusion. Which direction it will likely take in the future is unclear, but by considering internal criteria, some speculation is possible. New Classical economics was short-lived because it failed to meet the article and teachability criteria. New Keynesian economics, because it uses the same models as do New Classicals, faces many of the same problems that New Classical economics did; and unless it changes, it, too, is likely to be as short-lived. The typical New Keynesian model takes a New Classical model and demonstrates how, if one slightly modifies an assumption about information or about institutional constraints on individuals, the model leads to Keynesian results. That provides some easy dissertations and articles, but since there are limited New Classical models, there are limited possibilities for New Keynesians. There are only so many times you can show that the rational expectations assumption does not necessarily lead to equilibrium.

The New Keynesian school is, however, in a better position than the New Classical school in regard to teachability. It seems to have reached a compromise with neo-Keynesians. Advanced work is done using New Keynesian models; lower level textbooks teach neo-Keynesian models.[10] But this is a tenuous marriage which continues only because there is no better alternative.

If New Keynesian economics is to have staying power, it must develop some method to modify the simple textbook model to demonstrate and contrast its arguments and alternatives. To date it has not done so, and thus on internal criteria New Keynesian economics has a limited future.

The neo-Keynesian model is in a stronger position in regard to teaching, but it does not meet the article criterion. Unless the model evolves further and incorporates dynamic considerations, it, too, has a limited future. The historical approach has similar problems on the article criterion, but the confusion will likely allow more historical articles to be published than otherwise, especially if the articles can relate to modern developments.

My conclusion, then, is that even though Keynesian economics is in current disarray, its future, although uncertain as to the direction it will go, looks relatively strong in the short term, and somewhat less certain in the longer term. Because of its deep penetration into the textbooks, Keynesian economics will likely dominate the theoretical work of the 1980s and 1990s, but its domination will be nothing like the blissful days of the 1930s and 1940s.

Notes

1. Elsewhere (see Colander 1986) I have described these theories in more detail.

2. Obviously the issues are much more complicated than I can discuss in a short paper. External and internal criteria interact in complicated ways that I do not have space to capture.

3. There is a third set of criteria somewhere between internal and external criteria, and it consists of the "political" (how well does the theory fit political needs?) and "funding" (can economists get paid for working on their theory?) criteria. While these are interesting and relevant, because of shortage of space I do not deal with them here.

4. The importance of teachability depends upon the nature of the profession and the type of job researchers earn their money from. In the United States, most theoretical economists are teachers, hence teachability is extremely important. Moreover, the nature of the teaching method determines how that simple model must be reduced. As teaching methods change, a theory that was teachable may become unteachable.

5. These two revolutions threw off track another revolution which began in the 1930s—the development of monopolistic or imperfect competition—in part because they were both firmly based in Marshallian tradition. Off track, it simply died, with Joan Robinson forsaking her role in the imperfect competition revolution for Keynesian economics, much to the consternation of Edward Chamberlin.

6. This compromise is nicely described by Leijonhufvud (1968) in one of the works that furthered the theoretical breakdown of the neo-Classical–neo-Keynesian synthesis.

7. Although the Keynesian theory was not grounded in general equilibrium theory, attempts were made to give it a pretense of a general equilibrium grounding. Don Patinkin's real balance effect provided a semblance of general equilibrium grounding which, although incomplete and inappropriate from a formal general equilibrium standpoint, served the purpose of the time.

8. New Classical economists were not especially concerned with practice; it was a theoretical revolution. To the degree that it was concerned with practice, it simply borrowed monetarist policy prescriptions.

9. Having recently completed a macroeconomics textbook in which I tried not to focus on IS/LM analysis, I can attest from experience to the strong push by reviewers to structure macroeconomic books around IS/LM analysis. My compromise with the reviewers was a historical approach where I include IS/LM analysis, but it is not the only model presented.

10. A recent macroeconomic text (1986) by John Taylor and Robert Hall, whom I would call New Keynesians, presents the neo-Keynesian model as the core of macroeconomics and throws in discussions of New Keynesian propositions; they do not point out the problem in connecting the two.

7

Economic Methodology, Macroeconomics, and Externalities

We economists like to picture economics as a serious, or at least a disciplined, inquiry into economic phenomena: Economics is searching for economic truth, whatever that may be. I'm not about to enter into the question of whether economics is a science; I suspect it is reasonable to call economics a science, but justifying doing so would require a foray into heavy hermeneutical heuristics, something I, and no doubt the reader, would rather avoid. I'm also not going to discuss whether economics is a disciplined inquiry into economic phenomena; perusing almost any economic journal will assure the reader that it is. Searching for the truth is the last part of the picture, and that's the part I'd like to consider briefly in this essay.

Philosophers of science, at least in the part of their work that filters down to interested nonphilosophers of science, take it for granted that economists, and all scientists, search for the truth. Economic methodology follows that view; economic researchers may have trouble deciding what the truth is, but somehow, were it to be revealed to them, it would be the truth they were searching for. It is that proposition to which I object. If neo-classical economics' basic assumption is correct—that economists are rational maximizers—then it is incorrect to assume economists are searching for the truth. Neo-classical economists cannot hold the assumptions they do and their positivist methodology. One or the other must go.

Now, I believe that economists are rational—at least they are as rational maximizers as exist (they have assumed the process so much they actually use the process). What makes that last sentence nonobjectionable, or at least nondebatable, is our lack of knowledge of the nature of what people are maximizing. There is no accounting for tastes, and reasonable economists shy away from making normative judgments about individual decisions. Whether economists should avoid any assumptions about taste is debatable, but they avoid them anyway. Economic methodologists don't take such a hesitant role. They take the strong position that economists search for the truth, and that is why the economic methodology doesn't shed much light on what economists do.

I suggest that the best way to shed light on the current state of economics is to look at the economics profession through an economic lens. This approach requires giving up the assumption that economists search for the truth. What economists try to do is to maximize their welfare, not to search for the truth. Truth still plays a role, since for most economists the desire for truth is plausibly to be found in their utility function. However, I suspect that, given current institutions, it is relatively unimportant. My suspicion is that because empirical validation of economic theories is difficult, if not impossible, the desire for truth is probably to be found somewhere between a bowl of Wheaties and a glass of iced tea. The economists I talk to seem more interested in articles and publications (their own), teaching, promotion, puzzles, money, and sex, not necessarily in that order. With academic economists I know, these more mundane interests predominate. In this essay I focus on two of those interests, publication and teaching, and discuss how these interests have led to a model being taught to students that is pedagogically unsound and, quite simply, false.

It was actually my attempt to understand how this incorrect model entered the textbooks that led me to a consideration of methodology. I reasoned: If economists were interested in searching for or teaching the truth, they never would have let such a model become the central focus of what is taught to undergraduates.

Only after understanding what economists are trying to do can one understand why we're teaching a model—the aggregate supply/aggregate demand model—that is confusing and logically flawed and a step backward from earlier models. The current state of economics has come about by natural evolution in a set of institutions in which economists choose models that maximize their welfare.

The publication criterion dominates economists' interests early in our careers. As I discussed in the last essay, the Keynesian model and its derivatives provided sufficient conundrums that were sufficiently beguiling to keep journal editors happy. Most of the conundrums were never definitely answered, and, for many, the best answers were the earliest ones, but the formalization and expansion of the models kept graduate students and researchers in the money—and the models kept textbook writers and teachers in the money. Those were the Camelot days of economics.

The Camelot days ended in the 1970s; researchers left Keynesian macroeconomics as the rich article veins became exhausted. The models continue to play a role in teaching, but the inflation of the 1970s could not be easily modeled within the IS/LM (Investment = Savings/Liquidity = Money) framework. The reason inflation could not be easily modeled is also easily explainable: Inflation is a dynamic phenomenon, while the existing models were comparative static. Given that difference, there is no way inflation would fit with IS/LM models. No matter; the teaching criterion demanded that inflation be easily modeled, and textbook writers obliged. Economists' rational self-interest as seen in the teaching criterion overwhelmed not only the search for truth but also logical consistency.

What economists did at that point is to pull a sleight-of-hand and introduce an addendum to the model that made it seem as if they were analyzing inflation when, in fact, they weren't. The sleight-of-hand was accomplished by grafting the AS/AD analysis onto the Keynesian model. But the sleight-of-hand got out of hand, and the addendum replaced the analysis in introductory texts. But at that point everyone was too compromised to complain or to object.

AS/AD analysis, as presented in most textbooks, is, quite simply, a retrograde analysis that provides students with a crutch to make the average student think that he or she understands how inflation fits into the Keynesian model. But, in fact, the AS/AD model confuses an understanding of inflation with an understanding of the aggregate price level; moreover, it provides a worse explanation of the aggregate price level than did the quantity theory of money. It encourages students to understand incorrectly how aggregate disequilibrium forces operate. In short, it doesn't explain what it purports to explain (inflation); it doesn't even explain what it should appropriately purport to explain (the price level); and it leads to an incorrect explanation of how the aggregate economy adjusts.

For a long time I was at a loss to explain how this state of affairs came about and was at an even greater loss to explain how to get out of it. It was in puzzling about this phenomenon that I turned to economic methodology and came upon the above economic theory of methodology. The only explanation I could find that was consistent with the use of AS/AD analysis was that economists didn't care that the model didn't explain. It was teachable and that met their criterion.

The failure of AS/AD analysis would not be surprising to students from 1900 to 1970. No one then would have thought to use AS/AD analysis to discuss the aggregate economy. When graphical supply/demand analysis was first developed and became the staple of the teaching of economics, economists were very careful to limit its applicability to partial equilibrium analysis in which a movement along one curve would not cause a shift in the other curve. Otherwise (students were correctly taught), the analysis would be meaningless since there would be no disequilibrium adjustment mechanism to provide the necessary supplement to the comparative static analysis. For comparative static graphical analysis to be reasonable, there must be a way to move from disequilibrium to equilibrium without the curves shifting. In Marshall's supply/demand analysis, relative prices were on the vertical axis and the disequilibrium story that accompanied the graphical analysis, and gave it its power, relied upon the incentive effects that occurred when relative prices changed.

Partial equilibrium supply/demand analysis did so well by economists (it neatly met the teaching criterion) that when macroeconomics developed it, too, needed a comparable graphical totem. The Keynesian cross first served that function; the IS/LM cross was made an addendum at the intermediate level. Both of these had an accompanying disequilibrium adjustment analysis based on a modification of the Keynesian multiplier story: When aggregate supply was greater than aggregate demand, suppliers cut back production, reducing aggregate supply. That reduction further decreased aggregate demand, but, because the marginal propensity to expend was less than one, eventually the two would meet.

This adjustment story recognized the interconnection between aggregate supply and aggregate demand and made it central to the analysis. If there were an aggregate disequilibrium both aggregate supply and aggregate demand would shift. Because the marginal propensity to consume was less than one, eventually the shifting aggregate supply and aggregate demand would achieve an aggregate equilibrium. IS/LM analysis modified this disequilibrium adjustment story somewhat—interest rates could also adjust—causing changes in investment that would have a multiplier effect in the opposite direction, but the underlying disequilibrium story remained.

The introduction of a flexible price level modified the adjustment story even more: Changes in the price level would change the real money supply, which would change the interest rate, which would change investment, which would begin a multiplier effect in the opposite direction, further reducing the net adjust-

Figure 1.

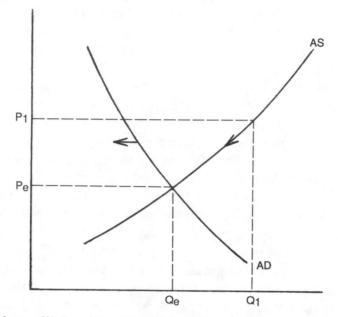

ment but still leaving the disequilibrium adjustment story in place. While there was debate about the speed and importance of the various adjustment processes, the underlying adjustment story was still there. (I should point out that all participants agreed that the real-world price level-real money supply adjustment was minimal—irrelevant to the checkerboard of real life.)

AS/AD analysis evolved from the modified flexible price IS/LM analysis so it would seem that it, too, should have an equivalent adjustment story to accompany it. But it doesn't. In the evolution the actual disequilibrium adjustment story that appropriately accompanies the analysis has been totally lost. It isn't presented in the texts, and the analysis is specifically designed in textbooks so that it looks to students as if a different adjustment process is taking place, one which is superficially satisfying to students but fundamentally wrong.

Consider the AS/AD diagram. Say we are in disequilibrium at price level P_1. The inevitable story I get when I ask students, and

Figure 2. **How Does the Economy Adjust from (Q_1 P_1) to (Q_e, P_e)?**

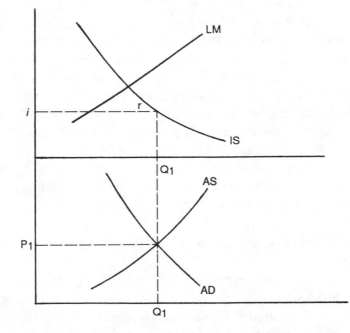

many faculty, is that the price level falls, quantity supplied decreases, and quantity demand increases—just as a fall in relative prices will bring about equilibrium in partial equilibrium analysis. That is not the correct adjustment process; the price level falling is not a reasonable disequilibrium adjustment mechanism. The economy simply doesn't work that way, and no theoretical economist I know believes it does work that way.

The disequilibrium story that would follow from the consumption function–IS/LM analysis would focus on the multiplier and the interaction of supply and demand. A shortage of expected aggregate demand causes firms to lay off workers—*decreasing* aggregate supply. That decrease causes a decrease in aggregate demand. In that story a movement along the supply curve shifts the aggregate demand curve. The equilibrium (Q_e P_e) is never reached; the final equilibrium depends on where one started. Put simply, the final equilibrium depends on the process of getting there; there may well be an equilibrium, but the AS/AD model is not going to show it to you.

Now, if AS/AD is not going to give you an equilibrium, how does it seem to do so in the IS/LM and AS/AD models? The answer is: It doesn't give you the correct equilibrium. Consider Figure 2, and assume that initially we are in equilibrium in the goods market, but in disequilibrium in the money market. Since AS and AD represent the goods market we must be in equilibrium in the goods market; therefore the AS and AD curves intersect at P_1 and Q_1. As we move to equilibrium, the AD curve shifts. But if, as it shifts, the price level changes, then the LM curve is going to shift; the final equilibrium is indeterminant. There are simply too many things changing for a two-dimension diagram to handle.

The Externality Approach to Macro

For reasons discussed in the first part of this paper, the forces to modify the AS/AD analysis are weak. The AS/AD model will be replaced only by another model, which provides an equally simple and superficially satisfying story.

Almost every economist I know, and every good economist I know (I define a good economist as one who accepts my argument), accepts my argument, but argues that AS/AD is simply a pedagogical tool and should not be taken too seriously. My response is that students take it seriously and deserve better. But I now recognize that the AS/AD model is here to stay. The question is how to amend it so that its errors are fewer and less likely to mislead students.

My suggested answer is paradoxical. It is that the one fixed curve in the system—the AS curve—is precisely the one that should be shifted. A downward-sloping IS curve is inconsistent with the current AS/AD models. Since the IS curve represents equilibrium points in the goods market, at each point on the IS curve aggregate supply and aggregate demand must be in equilibrium. Thus to model the adjustment process correctly we must show the interconnection between the AS and AD curves. To do so I propose an alternative distinction between the Keynesian aggregate supply curve and the Classical aggregate supply curve. The Keynesian AS curve shifts around following demand, because in the Keynesian system supply depends upon expected demand. This adjusting supply curve embodies the idea in the multiplier. Firms supply goods based on expectations of demand that are, in turn, dependent on actual demand. Such an expectation-based Keynesian AS curve is consistent with a downward-sloping IS curve: There are multiple equilibrium output levels.

It is this dependence of supply on expectations, not the assumption of fixed wages, that makes New Keynesian analysis different from the New Classical analysis. This dependence, and only this dependence, makes the analysis consistent with the basic Keynesian disequilibrium story. When there is excess supply, firms fire workers (at fixed wages and prices or at flexible wages and prices), lowering demand and supply and starting a multiplier effect.

The shifting AS curve can be justified in modern terms because embodied in the shifting AS curve is a macroexternality— neither individuals nor firms take into account the effect that their decisions will have on aggregate demand or aggregate supply. Equilibrium varies according to expectations, and multiple equilibria are possible.

It is my premise that this macroeconomics externality story is an appealing one. It is consistent with students' intuition, and it neatly differentiates New Classicals from New Keynesians. New Classicals believe that such expectational conundrums are of minor importance and assume them away in their models: individuals have rational, not reasonable, expectations and any macroeconomic externalities are assumed away. New Keynesians believe that such expectational conundrums are of major importance and make them central to their model.

In this short paper I haven't had time to develop the arguments fully, but it is my hope that the discussion stimulates teachers to expand upon it and avoid the unqualified use of AS/AD analysis.

4

Critics of Economics

8

Galbraith and the Theory of Price Control

I think most people who have read it would say that it is the best book I have ever written. The only difficulty is that five people read it. Maybe ten. I made up my mind that I would never again place myself at the mercy of the technical economists who had the enormous power to ignore what I had written. I set out to involve a larger community. I would involve a larger community. I would involve economists by having the larger public say to them, "Where do you stand on Galbraith's idea of price control?" They would have to confront what I said. (Galbraith 1967)

The "it" in the above passage is *A Theory of Price Control*, a book published in 1952 (1952b) and reissued in 1980 under the new title, *A Theory of Price Control: The Classic Account* (1980). Despite the addition to the title, it still seems fair to say that few economists have read the book, and while most economists are familiar with Galbraith's views on price controls (he favors them), few economists have seriously confronted what he had to say about controls or why he favors them. This lack of recognition is unfortunate. *A Theory of Price Control* is one of Galbraith's finest works and is laden with ideas so important that it is a travesty it has been lost. Thus, this essay. It considers Galbraith's theory of controls, the forces in the economy and the profession that kept the book down, and whether Galbraith made the "right" decision to carry his argument to the general public.

Background to Galbraith's Theory

In 1941 Galbraith wrote a draft design for price controls.[1] His interest in price controls was a natural offshoot of his earlier work, which included a book, *Modern Competition and Business Policy*, written jointly with Henry Dennison (Galbraith and Dennison 1938), and a paper, "Monopoly Power and Price Rigidities" (Galbraith 1936).[2] This early theoretical work, his interest in industrial organization, and his personality led to his appointment as deputy administrator of the Office of Price Administration.

Galbraith's initial draft for wartime price controls followed what he called the liberal line of thinking at the time.[3] It placed principal reliance on fiscal policy—severe taxation and enforced savings—with price controls and rationing confined to items of special wartime importance that were in short supply. Experience changed Galbraith, and soon after he took office it became apparent that his initial design was "technically and administratively unworkable." The problem was that spending greatly exceeded supply. Partial controls created tremendous inequalities since one firm's prices were another's costs and the number of products made decision making almost impossible. Soon after entering office, Galbraith modified his position and supported a general control of all prices.

After resigning his post under political pressure in 1943, Galbraith wrote two essays (1946, 1947) based upon his experience. *A Theory of Price Control* was written at Harvard in 1950–51 at the urging of the publisher, who believed there would be renewed interest in price controls to accompany the Korean War. It was based on his two earlier essays, although it had almost no discussion of the practical issues covered in those earlier essays.

At the same time, Galbraith was also writing *American Capitalism* (1952a). There are parallels in viewpoints between the two books. Both focus on the "noncompetitive" nature of the economy. However, whereas *American Capitalism* developed the concept of countervailing power as an alternative to competition,

A Theory of Price Control stayed more closely within the mainstream view. For example, in *A Theory of Price Control*, Galbraith takes it for granted that sectors of the economy are competitive and that countervailing power is one, but not necessarily the most significant, competitive force. In *American Capitalism*, countervailing power had expanded and replaced competition as the equilibrating principle of capitalism.

Galbraith's Theory of Price Control

Galbraith's book on price controls was primarily concerned with informal theory. Since almost no other economist had then (or has now) formally considered the theory of price controls, Galbraith's book remains the state of the art. Even Milton Friedman concedes as much. Friedman writes (Friedman 1977, p. 12):

> Galbraith deserves a good deal of credit for his independence of mind, for his diligence in trying to spread his ideas, and for an attempt to put intellectual content into some of them.
>
> I mean that seriously. For example, in one policy which is rather peripheral to his general body of thought, namely that of price and wage control, Kenneth Galbraith has the company of many other people—but so far as I know, he is the only person who has made a serious attempt to present a theoretical analysis to justify his position.[4]

The informal theory is in contrast to Galbraith's earlier, rather formal (for the period) consideration of monopoly power and price rigidities. Such a change in focus from formal to applied and informal theory was natural; the emergence of the war changed almost all economists' focus; Galbraith merely went further than most economists, and he did not return.

The novelty of Galbraith's work on the theory of price controls lay in the novelty of the question, not the answer. Whereas others had merely attempted to summarize past experience with controls, he attempted to generalize his understanding and experience. The two most important lessons were that the economy was not even close to being competitive, at least in the "perfectly competitive" way that many economists of the time thought of it, and that in a nonperfectly competitive economy controls can play a useful supplemental role to aggregate demand policy. If pushed, I suspect that many economists might have agreed with Galbraith on the first and a somewhat smaller number on the second, at least for the wartime period. However, most economists were not pushed and did not ask these questions: What role can controls play? Is there a general theory of price control? In fact, for most economists, the concept of a general theory of price control was so farfetched that the book was relegated to the "classic" file before it was even read.[5] After all, "good" economists knew then (and, alas, still know today) that price controls are bad.

The lesson most economists learned from World War II was that Keynesian aggregate demand policy worked. The fact that the expansion of aggregate demand had been accompanied by major controls over wages and price, and that it was only in such an environment that highly expansionary Keynesian policies worked, was lost on the majority of the profession, conservative and liberal alike. As Evsey Domar put it in an interview: "Inflation was simply not an issue that we considered." For the majority of the profession, the wartime experience was sui generis.[6] Galbraith was different; he did not lose sight of nor hide from the difficult questions of inflation, and he deserves major credit for asking the "right" questions.

The Disequilibrium System

Asking the right questions is no guarantee of right answers. To decide whether Galbraith's theory of price controls is useful, we need to consider what this seventy-five-page book said. Let us begin with its most insightful contributions. First, unlike most liberal Keynesians, Galbraith foresaw (in 1951) that the inflation problem was likely to be a chronic problem of the Post-Keynesian era. Galbraith writes (1952b, p. 9):

Inflation, more than depression, I regard as the clear and present economic danger of our times and the one that is potentially more destructive of the values and amenities of democratic life.

Moreover, he preceded both Edmund Phelps and Milton Friedman in clearly spelling out the "accelerationist" hypothesis. Galbraith (Galbraith 1952b, pp. 63–65) writes:[7]

> If prices and wages are uncontrolled, there is full scope for such interaction, and in the inflationary process this is almost certainly of critical importance. The upward thrust in prices which would result from an excess of demand . . . would be self-equilibrating were there no further interaction of prices and wages. In modern labor and product markets, such a price increase leads, on the one hand, to expanded wage income and to still further pressure on given supplies in the product markets and, on the other hand, via cost increases, to still further price increases. For this process to continue without limit, some continuing supplement to demand is necessary.

Galbraith's view of the vertical long-run Phillips curve not only preceded Friedman's and Phelps's; it was also more sophisticated than theirs. Both Friedman's and Phelps's vision related to a Walrasian economy, and equilibrium was thought to be a point where excess supply equaled excess demand.[8] Galbraith's vision took a wider view of the equilibrium; he saw unemployment and underutilized capacity (excess supply and demand) as an equilibrating force with the necessary level of excess supply dependent on the nature of the price-setting institutions. For example, Galbraith (Galbraith 1952b, p. 34) writes:

> Excess demand during the war was the counterpart of a buffer of unemployed resources, especially unemployed workers—the buffer that is necessary for price stability in the absence of price control. If markets are uncontrolled, any near approach to full employment of normally employed workers will lead, in a strong market, to price increases or wage increases followed by price increases.

The view of equilibrium not as a supply/demand equilibrium

but as an "excess supply equilibrium" is fundamental to an understanding of any theory of price controls. In the Phelps-Friedman view where excess supply and excess demand are equal in equilibrium, a combination of expansionary nominal demand and a general wage and price control system would merely cause most markets to be in excess supply. Rationing would be necessary. In some markets output might be expanded, but in an equal number of markets there would be shortages. As aggregate nominal demand expanded, the shortages would become general. In Galbraith's version, excess supply markets predominate in the non-price-controlled equilibrium. In the absence of price controls, accelerating inflation would set in before a "supply/demand" equilibrium—at what might be called the non-accelerating inflation rate of unemployment (NAIRU). Thus price control, or what we now call an incomes policy, by preventing that accelerating inflation, allows the economy to operate at a higher level of resource utilization than it could in the absence of price controls. Shortages would be minimal. In short, by stopping the interaction of wages and prices, price controls could lower the NAIRU. Galbraith (1952b, p. 64) argues:

> If prices and wages are controlled effectively, then the interaction of wages and prices cannot so act as an accelerant of the inflationary movement.

He further argues (1952b, p. 34):

> Under the disequilibrium system by contrast, it was possible to dispense with the buffer of unemployed resources which would have been necessary for equilibrium stability and to substitute, through surplus demand, a positive pressure on resource use.

Unfortunately, Galbraith's 1952 view of accelerating inflation and a long-run Phillips curve at less than full employment was lost not only by the profession, but also by Galbraith. In *American Capitalism*, countervailing power replaced the missing competition in all markets. The buffer of unemployed resources was lost as countervailing power maintained the economy at a euphoric equilibrium. Galbraith (1981, p. 284) recognizes this failing in *American Capitalism*; he writes:

> That a countervailing assertion of economic power is the normal answer to original economic power, I still wholly believe. But in 1952, carried away by the idea, I made it far more inevitable and rather more equalizing than, in practice, it ever is. Countervailing power often does not emerge. Numerous groups—the ghetto young, the rural poor, textile workers, women clerical workers, many consumers—remain weak or helpless.

These groups, forgotten by Galbraith in *American Capitalism*, are his buffer of unemployed resources in *A Theory of Price Control*, and in the absence of a system of controls their existence is necessary to prevent accelerating inflation.

Part of the reason Galbraith lost sight of the necessary buffer of unemployed resources is that he was so original that he simultaneously developed various ideas. For example, Galbraith preceded the profession not only in predicting the accelerationist hypothesis; he also preceded both John Hicks and Arthur Okun in recognizing the importance of classifying the economy into fixed-price and flex-price sectors. He writes (Galbraith 1952b, p. 26):

> Thus, there are markets when prices can be fixed, in face of a considerable excess of demand over supply, without formal rationing controls. There are some, however, where this cannot be done. One of the central tasks of price administration is to distinguish between the two.

This division is oftentimes useful and is a key element in understanding the application of controls. However, in development of a general theory of controls, this division obscures certain issues. It suggests that in some sectors competition is entirely absent, while in other sectors competition works instantaneously. Price controls have a role only in the fixed-price sector and involve merely administrating the administrators. As I will argue below, for discussion of a general theory of controls, focusing on this aspect of the economy obscures more than it clarifies.

In summarizing Galbraith's contribution to the theory of price controls, I think it is fair to say that he was far ahead of the profession in recognizing the importance of price controls to a well-functioning, workably competitive market economy. By the 1990s, I suspect that his prediction (1952b) that "the theory of price controls is fated to become one of the expanding universes of economics" will be belatedly fulfilled.

Shortcomings of Galbraith's Theory

It is not only because he was ahead of his time that Galbraith's work did not have a major impact. It was also because the work itself was incomplete and flawed, as seminal works often are. The tantalizing tidbits quoted above were not carried through in any systematic development. They were stated and often dropped, while less important concepts were discussed at length.

At best, *A Theory of Price Control* would be called a thesis abstract; it had a wonderful variety of ideas that would have taken years to fill in adequately. Important ideas were hidden and sometimes contradicted in other parts of the book. For example, as I stated above, in my view the key to a theoretical understanding of price controls is an understanding of the nature of "the excess supply equilibrium." A theory of controls must explain why a market economy arrives at this equilibrium and how it can be changed. Galbraith touched on these issues in his discussion of "the disequilibrium system," which he defined (Galbraith 1952b, p. 29) as a system in which:

> . . . the incentives and compulsions of an unplanned economy were supplemented or supplanted by three new forces for determining economic behavior. These were:

(1) a more or less comprehensive system of direct control over the employment of economic resources,

(2) a nearly universal control over prices, and

(3) an aggregate of money demand substantially in excess of the available supply of goods and services.

The theoretical question raised by the disequilibrium system is how is it possible to achieve more output than was previously forthcoming. If the economy is already at an approximate supply-demand equilibrium, then further sustained output increases are impossible; any expansion of demand with controlled wages and prices would merely lead to shortages.

Galbraith's answer to this question suggests an incomplete and contradictory understanding. At times, he seems to imply that market imperfections such as bilateral monopoly and counter-vailing power are the cause. His simple dictum: "You don't have to control prices that are already being controlled" is neat, but it suggests that the problem is in who sets prices. But unless one provides an explanation of why seller-set prices are at a supra-competitive level, who sets prices is irrelevant. The relevant question is: Are wages and prices in our economy set at supra-competitive levels? If they are, then there is a chronic problem of unemployment; if they are not, then, although markets will adjust slowly in disequilibrium, on average they will be in neither equilibrium nor disequilibrium. Seller-set prices, fixed prices, or even slowly adjusting prices will not necessarily generate supra-competitive prices. To generate a theoretical role for price controls, one needs to postulate an *asymmetry*—either in the price adjustment process or in the equilibrium price setting process. Only such an asymmetry can cause prices on average to be high, even in steady state equilibrium. Whether prices are temporarily fixed is only a side issue.

What I am arguing is that the fixed-price–flex-price division, while relevant to some issues, is not directly relevant to the theory of price controls. All markets are in some sense competitive (flex price) and in some sense noncompetitive (fixed price). A fixed-price sector is merely a very slowly adjusting flex-price sector. A role for price controls exists only if the prices in general are in some sense too high.

Galbraith correctly suggests that excess demand during the war was the counterpart of a buffer of unemployed resources, especially unemployed workers—the buffer that is necessary for price stability in the absence of price control. He further states (Galbraith 1952b, p. 34):

> Under the disequilibrium system it was possible to dispense with the buffer of unemployed resources which would have been necessary for equilibrium stability and to substitute, through surplus demand, a positive pressure on resource utilization.

Had Galbraith consistently carried through on this point, he would have called the normal state of affairs "the disequilibrium system," and the price-controlled economy "the equilibrium system." But he did not; paradoxically, his failing was not in being too novel; his failing was in remaining too tied to neo-classical economic concepts. By calling the price control state the "disequilibrium system" and the normal state "equilibrium," Galbraith gave far too much "equilibrium" to the status quo.

The key insight into understanding a theoretical role for price controls is to understand that in an aggregate "equilibrium" un-employed resources exceed overemployed resources. Such an equilibrium would be characterized by general supply rationing. Perhaps this is most important in the labor markets where jobs are effectively rationed among potential workers. But it can also be seen in the fact that most firms plan for excess capacity. Moreover, the same pressures toward supracompetitive prices exist in what are normally considered "competitive markets." For example, in agricultural markets, suppliers organize and push the prices above equilibrium via political pressure on govern-ment. Given an institutional structure, the "countervailing power" to such attempts at monopolization is a buffer of under-utilized resources.

In summary, I believe Galbraith's theory failed because, for all his good intentions, he remained too much the Classical economist to state clearly that such excess supply is the standard state of affairs, and, without a clear statement of fact, it is impossible to develop a theory of price controls. Because Galbraith did not clearly state his thesis, he allowed the economics profession to classify his criticism as minor, not describing a fundamental flaw in the nature of a capitalist society. Thus, economists could disregard his theory of price controls.

The Practical Problem of Price and Wage Controls

The question of price control concerns both theory and practical implementation. The practical problem of price controls is how to institute such a system of controls and simultaneously maintain the advantages of the market system. Galbraith (1952b, p. 74) correctly recognized this difficulty when he wrote:

> It is the administration of price control and its obscene politics, far more than its economics, which lead me to wish for a peaceful world in which price regulation refers once again only to a limited war between private utilities and government.

Major problems with the political administration of controls make the institution of a general system of administrative price controls unthinkable. However, when that is the only tool available, one naturally focuses one's theory on it. Galbraith saw the only form of controls as administrative controls and thus naturally focused on the fixed-price sector. Controlling prices in this sector was merely administering the administrator. In working out his theory he let that view of administrative feasibility affect his thinking about what the problem was and thereby obscured his theory of controls.

Incentive anti-inflation plans such as tax-based income policies (TIPs) allow one to think of a much wider range of controls. Such plans affect the speed of adjustment of prices and, in doing so, offset any asymmetry in the market. A 100 percent TIP tax on price increases is the equivalent to total control over prices. Taxes of lower percentage rates are a form of partial price controls. Because they allow partial controls and leave individuals free to adjust prices, TIPs integrate the control over prices with the market process. Wages and prices can still adjust, but they do so in a way that does not leave such a large buffer of underutilized resources as is required under our current institutions.

Why Galbraith's Theory of Controls Was Ignored

I suspect that economists have avoided the issue of price controls because the vision of the steady state conflict equilibrium that it conveys is so at odds with the steady state cooperative equilibrium that underlies neo-classical economic ideology. Had Galbraith stayed within the theoretical economists' mold, it is my belief that he had both the ability and the personality to have changed the underlying ideology. His 1952 decision to involve the larger community, while good for Galbraith, was bad for the profession. As events progressed, while few economists can ignore Galbraith's views, few have considered them in depth, and Galbraith's legacy is a variety of important ideas that were never integrated into economic theory, rather than a major new ''Galbraithian school'' of economics.

Figure 1.

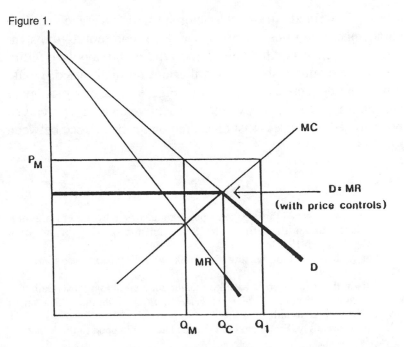

Note: A perfect system of price controls changes the demand curve to a perfectly elastic one. As can be seen in the figure, assuming the correct "price" is chosen, price controls reduce the level of monopoly in the economy and thereby both lower price and increase output. The argument is more complicated, but this simple exposition captures the essence of the theoretical pro-controls argument.

Appendix

The Theoretical Argument for Price and Wage Controls

It would be unfair of me to make such strong statements about Galbraith's supposed failing without being willing to put myself on the line. Elsewhere (Colander 1982; Colander 1985; Colander and Olson 1984), I have stated the argument in more detail, so here a summary will suffice.

First, because of the structural characteristics of the economy, there is asymmetric price adjustment, and second, supplier monopolies and cartels predominate over demander monopolies and cartels. Combined, these characteristics, on average, lead to supracompetitive prices. Thus, if we were representing the standard steady state equilibrium, some type of monopoly equilibrium, not the supply-demand equilibrium normally used, would be the correct representation. As in Figure 1, at this monopoly equilibrium, prices are above the competitive level and perceived underutilized resources exist measured by the difference between Q_M and Q_1.

Notes

1. The "draft" was a three-page response to an article by Alvin Hansen; it was published under the title "The Selection and Timing of Inflation Controls" (Galbraith 1941).
2. For a discussion of writing the book with Dennison, see Galbraith (1981).
3. This initial discussion is based on Galbraith's autobiography (Galbraith 1981), his introduction to *A Theory of Price Control* (Galbraith 1952), and a conversation with Galbraith.
4. Not surprisingly, Friedman (1977) adds later, "I happen to think that the analysis is wrong."
5. In the preface to the 1980 edition, Galbraith wrote that the book was favorably reviewed by Joan Robinson and Paul Samuelson. Unfortunately, I was unable to find either review; Joan Robinson (1952) did review *American Capitalism*, and Samuelson referred to the book in his text (1955). Galbraith stated that this reference is probably what he meant by "review."
6. Notable exceptions include Post-Keynesians such as Sidney Weintraub and Abba Lerner and some conservatives such as William Fellner.
7. Phelps (1970, pp. 126–30), in considering the historical precedents of the accelerationist view, cites others but does not cite Galbraith.
8. Phelps (1970, p. 136) initially saw excess supplies and excess demand being equal in steady state equilibrium. He has since recanted and, in a private conversation, stated that his earlier work was probably confused.

9

Tearing Down Economists' Worlds

The role of the mainstream economist is to build a paradigm; the role of the heterodox economist is to tear that paradigm down and to replace it with an alternative. The question this paper addresses is: How should one conduct a paradigmatic revolution? It is a relevant question because over the last fifty years, U.S. heterodox economists have not been too successful at tearing down, or even modifying, the mainstream paradigm. Despite repeated attacks by a wide variety of critics, mainstream economics has ensconced itself and flaunted the techniques, assumptions, and conclusions that have been the target of heterodox criticisms.

Because of past failures we can best look to history as a guide to how not to do it. Of course, this statement assumes that the goal of the revolution is to overthrow the existing world. I point this out because of an experience I had at Columbia in the late 1960s when I was arguing with the vice president of Columbia's chapter of Students for Democratic Society about what the appropriate strategy was to accomplish the changes he wanted. I was arguing against "trashing" and direct confrontation; he was arguing in favor. We exchanged views for a while, and then he made a point in favor of trashing to which I had no response: He had never been as turned on as after a confrontation and good sex is hard to come by.

This story springs to mind when I think about the role of

heterodox economists because it provides an explanation of many heterodox actions that makes those actions understandable to me. Heterodox economists seem to enjoy the process of confrontation much more than they worry about what they achieve through that confrontation. If that is the case, then the heterodox economist is not interested in tearing down the mainstream world but, rather, in living in an antiworld that exists only if the mainstream world exists. And if that is the case, no directions are needed; heterodox economists are succeeding completely.

This paper is addressed primarily to heterodox economists who are interested in achieving a result—tearing down and replacing the mainstream paradigm—and not to heterodox economists for whom the process is the result. How should he or she go about bringing on the revolution? But the paper also has a secondary goal and a secondary audience. That secondary goal is to stimulate discussion of the appropriate role of the heterodox economist, and the secondary audience is all economists. This broader audience is relevant because understanding the process by which ideas are spread is important to understanding the ideas that are spread and is itself an interesting, relevant, and unexplored field of study.

The paper is an unabashed example of neo-classical economic theory imperialism. It takes a utilitarian economic approach to the philosophy of science. Specifically, it argues that theories are not accepted because they are right or wrong; theories are accepted because they serve the purpose of the individual accepting a particular theory. (In economic terms the marginal benefits of accepting the theory exceed the marginal cost.)

I'm not arguing that the "truth" of a theory, or the ability of a theory to predict, does not play a role in what theories are accepted. It does as long as people get satisfaction, either monetary or psychological, from having discovered, or thinking they have discovered, truth. As long as truth is a component of scientists' utility function, either directly or indirectly, "true" theories will be accepted over "false" theories. What I am arguing is that the intellectual satisfaction about the truth or falsity or reasonableness of a theory is only one aspect of benefits and costs that concerns individuals. As, or more, important are the social and financial rewards for individuals working on that research program.

Applying this economic approach to the philosophy of science modifies Alfred North Whitehead's well-known maxim that a theory is replaced only by another theory. The economic equivalent to the maxim is: A world can be replaced only by another world. A world includes a theory, but it is much larger. It also includes the institutional and sociological aspects as well as the myths and stories which make that theory into a teachable subject and hence perpetuate that theory.

Having a better theory will not lead to its acceptance. One must have a theory that offers higher gains than does the existing theory. Intellectual satisfaction is one aspect of the gain, an aspect that has been widely considered by philosophers of science. In this paper I consider three other aspects of a theory that significantly contribute to those costs and benefits: publishability, teachability, and communicability.

For economics a new research program will be accepted only if it offers a better expected life for a majority of the 150,000 or so practicing economists out there. Put simply: If an economist cannot see a role for him or herself at least as important in the new world as the current role that person fills, the economist will probably continue operating in the old.

Following this approach, I believe that what we now call mainstream economics did not evolve into mainstream economics because it offered the best insight into economic processes, although the insights it offered clearly played a role in that evolution. Mainstream economics became the mainstream because it offered a set of activities for a wide variety of talents. For the abstract, creative thinker, it had "peaches waiting to be picked," as Samuelson (1964) put it, but it also had "oysters to be shucked" for most of us. It needed individuals to create tools, to transfer tools from other disciplines, but it also needed individuals to apply those tools, to carry out the more mundane tasks.

Initially, statistical work, and then econometrics, was extraordinarily important to the mainstream's success. It was important not so much for the empirical support it gave to the theory (that was rather minimal) but rather for the jobs it created for those in the ranks. Even if you had nothing to say, you could crank out a dissertation and enough papers so that you received tenure.

Talking to heterodox economists, I find that most of them are continually amazed at how mainstream economists won't even consider their arguments. Using my neo-classical economic theory of philosophy, they shouldn't be. Most individuals don't think about the world they're in. A person has a job and does that job. Most people are not creative; they don't create new worlds. They live in whatever world they inherit, as long as that world provides them with a minimum level of satisfaction. Any successful revolutionary research program must have meaningful jobs for these individuals.

Most heterodox thinkers haven't recognized that reality. They set forth a research program requiring an array of creative, insightful, nonparallel thinkers and then wonder why their ranks don't fill when, obviously, their new world is so much more intellectually satisfying than the one they want to leave behind. The examples are legion. Thorstein Veblen was brilliant, but he would have left little to no legacy had it not been for others, such as Wesley Clair Mitchell, who provided tasks for normal economists who were sympathetic to Veblen to perform. Consider four other, more recent, economists and their legacies: Lerner, Galbraith, Friedman, and Samuelson.

Neither the economist J.K. Galbraith nor Abba Lerner has made much impact on the profession, despite their teaching abilities, their insights, and their lives. The reason is that they offered nothing for their graduate students to do. Hence each had few propagators of his theory. Both shunned statistical work, or even modeling, and these are what provide possibilities for less creative researchers. To write under Abba Lerner meant to write something meaningful; few people wrote under Lerner.

Milton Friedman, on the other hand, offered students possibilities: applying simple Marshallian models to markets, estimating consumption functions and demand for money curves. Friedman succeeded in large part because his program fulfilled their publishing needs. Similarly, Paul Samuelson was extraordinarily inspired, but his influence derives as much from the set of doable, unfilled tasks he has left in his wake as from the inspiration with which he was endowed. Mathematical modeling was, and remains, solid drone work. Mathematical economics, once one learned the economics, had a number of grind-them-out dissertations and papers. It doesn't matter that much of that work was of dubious value; it is work and it allows the solid core of Friedmanites and Samuelsonians to populate the economics world. Lerner, by contrast, offered no drone work.

It is my hypothesis that had Samuelson and Friedman also required their students to make their models meaningful they would have had almost no students, because they would have been requiring a higher level of skills than most students have.

Publishability

The existence of a set of tasks in a theory becomes important because of the nature of the U.S. institutions that provide employment for U.S. economists. Put simply, a revolutionary army travels on its stomach, and a paradigmatic revolution travels on its journals, which devour paper, which leads to tenure and promotion.

The nature of the existing institutions plays a central role in determining an acceptable research program. The U.S. economics profession is academically dominated; to succeed, U.S. economists must write dissertations and journal articles. Successful economists publish. Were the profession dominated by business or government economists whose needs are different, a successful research program would be quite different. Similarly, were the tenure system changed, the nature of the appropriate research program would change.

Considering these institutional criteria provides insight into the evolution of mainstream economic theory over the past seventy-five years. In micro, Marshallian economics won out over the then-existing broad generalities because it offered sets of jobs for researchers—explaining elasticity, graphical analysis of taxes, tariffs, and costs. Far more sophisticated and insightful work, like that of Frank Ramsey, was forgotten until it was rediscovered in the 1960s and 1970s once the techniques improved.

Marshallian economics ended when the simple conundrums within a partial equilibrium framework were explored and replaced with Walrasian economics, with new, more complicated, conundrums for researchers to explore and write papers about.

The Keynesian revolution was successful for the same reasons that the Walrasian paradigm was. It fulfilled the internal needs of its soldiers; it provided numerous dissertation and article topics, as can be seen by the outpouring of simple models that filled the journals in the late 1940s and early 1950s. In these early years the simultaneous development of national income accounts and econometrics led to an enormous number of empirical questions the new theory could explore and answer.

Through the mid-1960s, the evolution of macro models was sufficiently fast to offset the diminishing returns in article production, keeping article topics relatively easy to come by for new researchers. Articles continued to flow from the models relatively easily as the simple consumption function model of the 1950s evolved into the IS/LM model, with its numerous variants and conundrums, and then into the IS/LM-aggregate supply/ aggregate demand models in the 1960s and 1970s. But it was becoming more and more difficult to think of topics, and hence by the late 1970s the time was ripe for the New Classical–New Keynesian revolution.

Teachability

The U.S. academic institutional structure also makes a second criterion of a theory important: It must be teachable. Teachability depends on the teacher and the institutional setting. In the United States, this institutional setting requires what might be called mass-teachability. A theory must be amenable to being reduced to multiple-choice questions and simple models that have nice stories associated with them. Marshallian economics, with its graphical, partial equilibrium, supply demand analysis, serves the purpose well, and hence it remains the core of the undergraduate teaching in micro, even though in graduate schools it has been replaced by general equilibrium Walrasian theory and highly mathematical dynamic search models.

Heterodox analysis generally scores poorly on mass teachability. For example, the Austrian market-process analysis provides a good, appealing story, but it does not have a nice simple model to go along with it. Given the right teacher, it can be taught, but it can't be mass-taught in packaged textbook analysis, and hence it remains outside of the textbooks.

Keynesian economics also nicely met the teachability criterion. It was eminently reducible to simple, neat models, as is demonstrated by the rapid acceptance of Lorie Tarshis's (1947) and Paul Samuelson's (1948) texts which provided simple models of Keynesian thinking. It was irrelevant that the models were not as insightful as others, such as Dennis Robertson's approach of analyzing sequence economies. Robertson's analysis was too difficult to teach. Even today, after Keynesian models have been discarded on the high theoretical level, they form the basis of what is taught at the beginning and intermediate levels of macroeconomics.

Communicability

Other institutional criteria relevant to a theory's acceptance include its ability to be communicated to the general public via the press. This is one area where mainstream economics is weak; but heterodox economics is not much stronger. Some groups have press forums—such as supply-side economics having an in at the *Wall Street Journal*—but Institutionalists or Post-Keynesians seldom talk directly to the public. When they have communicated directly to the public—as Galbraith has, for instance—they have not used that as a podium to increase their communication to the profession, and, for Galbraith at least, that omission reduced his influence in the profession.

Social and Political Considerations

Besides institutional criteria determining a theory's acceptability, the social and political criteria also play roles. Heterodox economists must consider these criteria in trying to get their views adopted.

I am not suggesting an unfriendly adversarial political role. That will simply galvanize the mainstream opposition. Rather, I am suggesting a friendly adversarial political role.

There are enormous possibilities for heterodox influence in American Economics Association politics, but the AEA remains a mainstream-controlled organization. This underrepresentation of heterodox economists means that heterodox economists don't get on panels, boards, or decision-making committees. Yet it is these panels, boards, and committees that lead to tenure and advancement. The same political issues hold within the university. Academic institutions are political entities controlled by extraordinarily bright individuals, many with tenure, who have enormous amounts of time to devote to political and administrative infighting for that control. Unless one gains control, one's revolution will be short-circuited. A paradigmatic revolution consists as much of fighting these political battles as it does of fighting the battle of ideas.

Closely related to political criteria are social issues. Heterodox economists are often treated unfairly, harshly; their criticisms are not seriously considered. This idea gap frequently leads to a social gap as well; heterodox economists don't interact with mainstream economists. In my view, this is not the best strategy. The successful revolutionary will ignore such attacks; developing a chip on one's shoulder because of such practices serves no purpose. Ideas are not rethought from reading learned papers. Ideas are rethought because of a conversation over drinks—or on a ski trip. Thus socially, heterodox economists should be spies from within—indistinguishable from mainstream economists.

Let me give you an example of a member of the Virginia school. Gordon Tullock is a very nice person. He will be bothered that I say this, and I am sure he will go out of his way, the next time I see him, to try to prove me wrong. But deep down he really is a very nice person.

In his writing and in his interaction with administrators and other economists he hid this quality well, and he did what he could to make people believe him to be mean and nasty. He was so successful that he was forced to leave the University of Virginia. He has still made a significant mark on the profession, but had he not hidden his inherent niceness, he likely would have left a much deeper mark.

As important as communicating with mainstream economists is communicating and socializing with other heterodox economists. I am amazed to find so little attempt at understanding among various heterodox groups when their goals are often so similar. A revolution will be successful only if diverse heterodox groups work together.

Social and political actions are not sufficient. The only way these social and political actions will work is if the heterodox economist has a mastery of the ideas and techniques that he or she is tearing down. Taking potshots at a world without a deep understanding of that world and the reasons it is the way it is serves little purpose. Thus a good heterodox economist must understand both the thought and the sociology of the profession.

Having briefly outlined my revolutionary agenda, I hope I have made it clear why most revolutions fail. Revolutions aren't sexy; they aren't exciting; they require a type of selfless dedication that our society doesn't foster and that seems, as a personality trait, to be inconsistent with an individual's taking a heterodox position. Thus while the mainstream thought is, in my view, ripe for revolution, it seems more likely to rot from within than to be plucked by a heterodox group.

10

Form and Content in Appraising Recent Economic Developments

The subjects of this paper are two interrelated questions: What is the role of the historian of economic thought in discussing and appraising current developments in economics? What are the appropriate methods for studying these developments? My thesis is that the historian of economic thought has an important role to play in discussing and appraising current developments, but that the role is of a different nature than is his or her role in the study of history. Therefore, the methods—the tools and means of analysis—are different. Specifically, I argue that historians of recent economic thought, in addition to the literary exegesis and archival methods, must rely heavily on interviewing, surveying, and bibliometric methods.

Since the contrast I am making is between "history" and "current developments," I should make clear what I mean by these terms. The term "history" conveys a sense of events sufficiently removed so that the historian can bring a historical perspective to his or her analysis. While there is no specific time period associated with an event's becoming history, a possible demarcation is the time period after which all the participants are dead. Thus something that happened a hundred years ago is history, and something that happened in the last five years is likely to be a current development. Following that demarcation, economic historians have predominantly focused their attention on the history of economic thought, and the field is called "history of economic thought" rather than "development of economic thought."

The reasoning for concentrating on history goes as follows: Current developments are not history and when considering such developments one necessarily lacks perspective that historians studying true history have. While I agree with this argument, I do not believe it means historians of thought should not study and appraise current developments. It simply means that they must replace the historical perspective with an alternative perspective, within the use of which they have a comparative advantage.

Recent developments in the profession of economics have increased the need for historians of thought to take on this role of appraising current developments. In the teaching of graduate economics, the profession has deemphasized literature and interpretation, emphasizing tools instead. Similarly in articles: whereas there once was a mandatory broad review of literature section, that literature review is narrowing. Much of the mainstream profession has eliminated any consideration of the context of their work, either within various schools of thought or within recent literature. In a survey of graduate schools done by Arjo Klamer and myself (1987; see also pp. 41–62), only 10 percent of graduate students believed that a knowledge of economic literature was very important to being "on the fast track" as an economist, while 43 percent thought it unimportant.

This contextual void of current research leaves an opening for historians of thought to exploit their comparative advantage and provide additional insight into current developments in theory. In doing so they need not address the often-heard criticism of history of thought nicely captured by Alfred North Whitehead's comment that "a science which hesitates to forget its founders is lost." The role of historians of recent thought is not concerned with its founders; that role is simply to get the profession to know its current practitioners and to get them to communicate with one another.

Historians of thought generally have failed in this role. Much of the work on current developments done by historians of thought has been unappreciated by the profession; their articles seldom appear in the top journals, and their articles on current economic theoretical issues in history of thought-oriented journals are seldom read and little referred to by mainstream economists. This is sad, not only for the ego of the historian of modern thought, but also for the profession, because a critical need in the profession is not being fulfilled.

It would be easy to blame the mainstream profession for the situation; mainstream economists, after all, are the ones who purged literature from their articles and the profession. But blaming the profession is not going to change reality. Instead, I think historians of thought must blame themselves, not because that is where the blame lies (that's an irrelevant question) but because that is where they can do something about the situation.

Historians of thought are to blame because they have sent students to work on recent subjects without giving them a clear sense of the set of tools that they can use to analyze current subjects. In the absence of such a guide, students have had to rely on the work of previous historians of thought as guides. Unfortunately, the work depends on having historical perspective, and in considering current events we *do* lack historical perspective. The contribution of historians of thought to analyzing current developments in theory can only be useful if they provide an alternative perspective (other than a historical perspective) that complements the theorists' perspective.

Form and Content

Historians of recent thought face a twofold problem. First, they must design a good product that complements mainstream economics; second, they must convince mainstream economists of its value.

Analyzing current developments and problems in theory using historical methodology is the way not to solve both problems.

Interpretive articles discussing the implications of, the method-ological jumps in, and the implicit values of a theory, while comparing and contrasting various theorists, is not the appropri-ate methodology for a historian of recent thought to use. This statement is independent of the content of the work; the work may be a superb product, and thus it may or may not solve the content problem, but that is irrelevant because these methods definitely fail to solve the second problem and thus will not sell. The form must be right for the content to be considered.

The "content" issue is a complicated one, and one must judge for oneself whether an article has, or does not have, valid points. I believe that there is important content in many of the analyses of current developments by historians of thought. But even if there has been good content in the argument, it will have no effect on the profession. The reason is that regardless of what I believe, there is a strong presumption held by mainstream econo-mists that articles by historians of thought on methodology and current developments have little content.

Most good theorists know, or think they know, when they are making methodological jumps; they know, or think they know, the implications and limitations of their model. They don't talk about these issues because, given the sociology of the profession, that is not something a theorist does. Moreover, they do not want to read or debate with others who do want to write or talk about these issues. They see themselves as scientists who want to get on with the business of doing science.

For a mainstream researcher to place himself or herself outside a small area of research and to assess and appraise that research would involve enormous hubris. The only activity that would involve more hubris would be for someone who is not a main-stream theorist to assess that research. Forget that this latter view follows from an even higher level of hubris, because it is based on a belief that if a theorist wanted to do so, he or she could write an article that would duplicate, and most likely surpass, anything a historian of thought could write, especially a young one who has not moved out to pasture after having been a "theorist."

Young theorists do not write such articles because doing so would violate the allowable form of discussion, with which theoretical points may be made within the economics profession, and they certainly are not going to read any nontheorist who violates these norms.[1]

Having been a reviewer for a variety of history of thought-oriented journals and being an avid consumer of appraisals of recent work, I could give a legion of examples of such articles without readership. But I have no need to pick on others' work. I can establish my credibility as knowing what does not work by using examples from my own work. When I first learned about rational expectations applied to macroeconomics in the mid-1970s, I, and now I suspect many others, saw the limitations and implications inherent in it. I wrote an article explaining these and relating rational expectations to the literature; I went around telling people my insights. The insights were greeted with yawns and with questions such as: Do you have a formal model? The papers were rejected by the top journals. One of the papers (Colander 1979) finally was published in a conference volume (a primary outlet for such a piece) and was little read; a second (Colander and Guthrie 1980–81), despite a great title, "Great Expectations: What the Dickens Do Rational Expectations Mean?" was published in the *Journal of Post Keynesian Economics* and soon forgotten, even by readers of the *JPKE*.

Similar experiences with unpublished papers on the difference between the NAIRU and the natural rate, the implications of implicit contracts, the implications of the market anti-inflation plans, and the limitations of optimal taxation analysis have finally made the point to me. The market for appraisal is small.

Now one might argue that the content of these papers was flawed—that my "insights" were not good insights and deserved to be forgotten. I strongly believe that content failure was not my problem, and I encourage all who are dubious to consider my unpublished papers.[2] My papers were disregarded because I "cheated"; I violated form, and the profession is loath to allow such violations.

Subsequent discussion with well-known economists has led me to the conclusion that the articles I wrote were articles that a number of theoretical economists could have written. Most of the arguments I raised and the methodological problems I pointed out were not new to them, although my ego still has me believe that others may not have thought of the problems in the particular way that I did. In Alfred Marshall's wonderful phrase, they were issues kept in the back of the mind. So by good mainstream economists my work was seen as pedestrian even though they might agree that the arguments I was making were sound and had not previously shown up in the literature. According to the standard practice of the profession, the only economists who are allowed to write such interpretive articles are the grand old men and women of the profession who have paid their dues by playing the formal game.[3]

I escaped the fate of most of those who violate the profession's norms. I was "discovered" by a famous economist, Abba Lerner, who had no sense of the profession's (or society's) norms. He went around telling people that the work I was doing deserved to be read. Out of professional courtesy and respect for Abba, some in the profession began to consider my work, especially that which was jointly done with Abba. Once he died, the interest waned, but by then I had a distinguished chair (albeit at an undergraduate college) and hence had made it to that status of "grand old man" from which I am allowed to comment. I still am little listened to, but I am no longer seen as a "cheat."[4]

As I stated at the beginning, I believe historians of thought have an important role to play in appraising theory. There is no invisible hand of truth to ensure that all the pieces of the theoretical puzzle fit together. Somebody has to define what the puzzle should be. But I also believe that mainstream economists have a point. Young historians of thought who have not participated in the development of the theory are not the best people to establish what the important issues are; current researchers who are simultaneously interested in appraisal and interpretation, who have both the narrow perspective of a researcher and the wide perspective of a historian of thought are the ideal people to do it. I also believe that it would be nice if elephants could fly. Until they do, there is a role for the historian of thought (even young ones) to play in analyzing and appraising recent theory. Thus, I turn to the second question: How to do it?

How Form Can Provide
the Missing Perspective

In appraising current developments in theory, all the historian's tools and methods are still necessary. They are not, however, sufficient for the historian of recent thought. How insufficient depends on the individual. For current researchers, or grand old men and women, literary exegesis combined with logic and good writing is sufficient; when John Hicks wrote, people listened. For all others, that approach is insufficient, even if it involves a complete mastery of all the articles and issues in the field. These others need a set of tools to provide them with the missing perspective; the tools substitute for, or at least complement, their reflective judgment. Content follows form. The writer is not appraising; the writer is simply using a set of tools. (The interrelation between the tools and the appraisal is obviously much more complicated, since the writer's appraisal shows through in the tools, but at least there is some separation of the writer and the appraisal, and that separation provides the needed perspective.)

It is important that we find different methods. As I stated above, the profession needs historians of thought to provide the insights, appraisal, and interpretation because the grand old men and women are becoming less grand as the narrowing process continues and literature is purged from the subject matter of journal articles.

The three methods I consider in this paper are interviewing, surveying, and bibliometrics. There may be others, but, I argue, these three should be part of the tool kit of every historian of recent economic thought. None of these methods is a stand-alone method. The information derived from these methods is not always accurate and is often contradictory. To get the most helpful information *one must know the literature*. Thus, these methods do not replace knowledge of literature; they complement it.

Interviews

The advantage of interviews is twofold. First, in the process of interviewing, the profession's interest in one's work is piqued; its members want to know what they and others have to say but are forbidden by the profession to talk about in articles. In asking questions of mainstream theorists, historians of thought become natural allies of the scholar being interviewed and are seen as people who are complementing the theorists' work, not duplicating it. One of the things that has amazed me as I have interviewed scholars is how open they are and how much they want to convey their ideas. Second, and most important, interviewing adds the missing perspective; interviews replace one's perspective with the researcher's perspective. Thus the hubris charge is avoided. I would argue that all appraisal of current research by historians of thought should make extensive use of interviews. The argument can be made even stronger: Any appraisal work by someone who is not doing the actual work himself or herself and that does not use interviews is seriously flawed.

Imagine that the possibility of interviewing Adam Smith or David Ricardo were opened to a historian of thought. The questions one could ask! How important are the existing set of institutions to your invisible hand argument? Under what conditions will your theory of value break down? If interviewing were possible and the historian did not interview, the historian's work would be considered incomplete. For historians (in my sense) such questions are impossible; they must deduce the answers to their questions from archival study—textual analysis of the writings, files, and letters of the economists in question. But that is a second-best approach. Historians of recent thought do not face these limitations; they can simply ask the producers of the idea they are studying—either by letter or in face-to-face interviews.

And in the process they can play an important role in the development of theory.

Two examples of successful work using the interviewing technique are the appraisal of general equilibrium analysis by Roy Weintraub (1986) and the analysis of New Classical economics by Arjo Klamer (1983). Weintraub, while not a grand old man, was already relatively well known and had made contributions to the literature. He was also the son of a distinguished economist and was making an argument that was sympathetic to mainstream economists—that the general equilibrium research program is progressive. Thus he had a number of things going for him. His looking at the broader issue was as close as we are likely to get to elephants flying.

But even these advantages were, I believe, insufficient to make Weintraub's appraisal of interest to the mainstream. His work interested them because of its form, not its content. His article and book on appraising general equilibrium analysis made extensive use of letter interviews. These letter interviews formed the basis of his article in the *Journal of Economic Literature* (March 1983) and the central chapter of his book, *General Equilibrium Analysis* (1985, chap. 6). Moreover, his methodological analysis was written as if it were an interview, and his analysis of the development of an article was a self-interview.

Klamer's *Conversations with Economists* (1983) provides a better example of the importance of form. Klamer did not have Weintraub's advantages, but his book, a collection of interviews of macroeconomic theorists, elicited enormous interest. His use of the interviewing technique played an important role in that interest. Had he made the same points by simply writing them or by reference to various economists' work, his book would have been disregarded.

Given the importance of interviews, part of the training of a historian of recent economic thought should be in interviewing techniques. Despite the fact that an enormous amount of literature exists on how to interview, currently techniques of interviewing are not taught.[5]

Surveys

A second technique seldom used by economists but useful in providing information about recent economic thought is surveying. Surveys are a way of interviewing large numbers of individuals without direct contact with them and getting quantitative results that can be easily summarized. Since surveys are a form of interviewing, like interviewing they provide the lacking perspective in analyzing recent developments. As with the interview, surveying complements the economic theorist and does not challenge him or her. Thus economists, while disparaging surveys, are generally interested in the results, especially since these results can be quantified.

My own experience with surveying provides a good example. As I distributed a survey, my former advisor asked what I was doing, and when I told him, he asked if I had left the economics profession. However, after Arjo Klamer and I (1987) tabulated the results of the survey, there was an enormous interest. Three economic journals asked if we were interested in publishing the results with them. Had we written an article based on a literature survey making the same points, it is unlikely we would have found any interest in our work.

Despite the existence of an enormous amount of literature on surveying techniques—how to structure questions to extract the information one wants while not biasing the results; how to increase response rates; how to interpret and organize the results of a survey—surveying is not taught to future historians of economic thought. Thus, while there have been some surveys done by economists who are historians of recent economic thought, the technique remains largely untapped.

Bibliometrics

A third method that should be part of the standard tool kit of the historian of recent economic thought is bibliometrics—the use of bibliographic information as data. The advantage of using bibliometrics is that it provides a quantification of what other-wise is an impression. An example of some interesting use of bibliometrics is a paper by Terry Plum (1987). In this study he quantifies and documents the movement of supply-side econom-ics from the popular press to the economic journals and traces its rise and fall in popularity. Much of what he found was known, but he added a quantitative dimension to that knowledge.

The reality facing a historian of recent thought is that the profession will consider the implications of his or her work only if that work adds something to what the profession believes it already knows. Quantification of general impressions does this: It adds information to what mainstream economists have and thus becomes of more interest to them.

Similar arguments can be made for citation and cocitation analysis. While these analyses have been more frequently used by historians of economic thought (e.g., Stigler 1982), they are not as widely used by historians of economic thought as they could be. For example, citation studies can be used with cluster analysis to create a map of schools of economics (McCain 1984).

While the use of these bibliometric techniques is not limited to the analyses of recent events, the burgeoning literature and the significant increase in on-line data bases make the use of these techniques especially applicable for the historian of recent thought. They help provide the perspective that is lacking in studying current developments.

The Texts of Textual Analysis

Despite my advocacy of the use of supplemental techniques, I still believe that textual analysis will continue to form the basis of the methods of the historian of economic thought. Techniques can provide a readership if one has something to say, but one will have something to say only if one knows the literature, and knowing the literature requires textual analysis. But here, too, the analysis of recent ongoing events differs from the analysis of historical events. The reason has partly to do with the currency of the work being studied and partly to do with the changing technology of disseminating information. The "currency" reason is obvious. The primary data source for the latter are the archives— the files saved by past economists. Historians of recent thought do not have archives, but they do have the working papers of leading economists, who are often delighted that anyone should be interested in their thought processes. If asked, many will supply various versions of their articles on their way to publication. Thus, simply to parallel the work of the historian, the historian of recent economic thought must analyze working papers, not only published articles.

But there is also a less obvious reason for not focusing one's analysis on articles. The 1950s represented an enormous change in the way economic ideas are disseminated. With the advent of the Xerox machine, journals and books become less the media of debate and more the "tombstones" marking one's role in a debate. Published articles have become "perfected articles." The thought processes, the arguments and false starts that give the analysis contextual meaning, are not to be found in the published articles. Thus in studying recent history, historians of thought should not concentrate on published papers. Early drafts and working papers are where the action is in the development of economic thinking, and to a large extent these should be the sources of much of the recent economic historian's textual analysis.[6] A good historian of recent economic thought will become part of the informal prepublished discussion network, thereby gaining wider access to publication and integrating his or her perspective into mainstream economic thinking.

Conclusion

Mainstream economics has entered into a contextual void because of its overconcentration on tools; historians of recent thought point this out often. Historians of recent thought have made the opposite mistake. In their training there is almost no consideration of tools, and the result is a contextual mess. Most historians of recent economic thought think that the economics profession has a problem; it is more helpful to see it as a problem of the historian of recent economic thought.

Most economists now agree that current graduate economic training is superb at training economists how to answer questions but poor at teaching economists which questions to ask. That is precisely the role that a good historian of recent economic thought should play. He or she should pinpoint unanswered questions, highlight the limitations in technique, and suggest connections in the literature that the more narrow researcher is likely to miss.

Historians of economic thought have something to add to current debates but must do it in a way that the profession will listen to. Each of the techniques described has its problems. People being interviewed shade reality to suit themselves; surveys are often biased and provide incomplete information; and bibliometrics is subject to serious abuse. My argument is not that these techniques should replace textual analysis; it is simply that they should be part of that analysis. Capturing as moving and amorphous a reality as current developments requires one to use all the tools he or she can.

Notes

1. I have become somewhat cynical about the internal dynamics of the profession. Initially, I believed that researchers searched for knowledge (or at least tried to discover what is false). I have since come to believe that researchers have a more complex utility function; discovering truth is one element, but most researchers don't ask questions of truth; they simply do what they are taught, working on their piece of the puzzle, with the implicit belief that the invisible hand of truth will put together the puzzle and lead to knowledge.

Students who are attracted to the history of thought, of whom I am one, generally have a different approach to understanding. They try to understand the entire puzzle, assuming that the pieces can be fitted together. Thus they push to show broader relationships and continuities outside of the formalism of the models. They generally deal with broad-brush language rather than narrow-brush mathematics. Bi-economists, who can go either way, generally favor the narrow-brush mathematics. They recognize that the broad-brush approach destroys the game that the profession has developed—a game that slows the way in which the pieces of the puzzle can be put together over a long period of time.

These institutional constraints on conveying knowledge are unlikely to change; they decrease the human capital depreciation of the knowledge that economists have learned and thus may serve useful internal rent-seeking functions for members of the profession.

2. If anyone actually wants to consider the unpublished papers, I'd be happy to send them after I dig them out of the deep recesses of my files.

3. In a wonderful letter to one of my coauthors, Axel Leijonhufvud jokingly told us this early on, suggesting that we save our insights for our AEA presidential addresses. It took a few more rejected articles for us to heed his advice.

4. The above discussion was not meant to elicit sympathy, or lambaste the profession; it was simply meant to establish my credentials in arguing that history of thought methodology applied to current developments doesn't sell.

5. Reducing that literature to its simplest components, the rules of interviewing are the following: (1) know the period and the literature; (2) work out a set of questions that will be likely to elicit the information you want; (3) let the person talk.

Much of the literature of interviewing concerns what I call adversarial interviewing, in which the interviewer is trying to elicit information the interviewee does not want to provide. That is not the type of interviewing that I am suggesting. I am suggesting nonadversarial interviewing in which the interviewer and interviewee become partners. They are trying to understand what role the interviewee played in a certain area. In my interviewing I make it clear to all my subjects that they will see the material and can change their words and meanings before the material is published.

6. Some have argued that historians of recent thought should be trained in literary criticism. I have no objection to that, but judging from the deconstructionist textual analysis that I have seen, these techniques are unlikely to get the historian of thought read by the economics profession.

11

In Defense of
Mainstream Economics

Mainstream economics has significant problems and should be changed. Much of it is irrelevant—the celestial mechanics of a nonexistent world, to use Ken Boulding's phrase. Its empirical foundations and testability criteria are suspect (Leamer 1988; Dewald et al. 1986); it has a fetish for sophisticated econometric techniques and an almost total disregard for simpler approaches to empirical evidence. In short, it often studies the wrong issues with the wrong tools and provides far less understanding than it should.

These criticisms are ones I suspect I share with most critics. Where I part company from the critics is in what to do about them. I believe in working from within the profession to change and redirect mainstream economics. Most critics want to replace it. (Critics who simply criticize and offer no proposals cannot be taken seriously.) My reasons for preferring working from within are:

• Despite the serious problems with mainstream economics there is much good in it; it is not clear that the "good" could be retained after any major departure from it.

• Mainstream economics is "institutionally successful"; it provides jobs for economists and work for researchers, and it commands a greater degree of respect than any of the other social sciences.

• The alternatives are not viable; even if the critics could correct some of the mainstream's problems, in doing so they would create other, more serious, ones.

Before I discuss these points, I should say what I mean by "mainstream economics." By "mainstream economics" I mean the central concepts and tools that are taught to students of economics, together with economists' research and mode of doing research. These include three general areas: microeconomics, macroeconomics, and econometrics. In microeconomics the central concept is that of rational economic decision makers optimizing; microeconomics considers the implications of that process of maximization for society as individuals interact. Competition and the invisible hand of the market play large roles in that interaction. On the undergraduate level these issues are studied in a Marshallian framework and the tools are primarily algebra, simple calculus, and geometric devices such as indifference curves, supply and demand curves, and the Edgeworth box. On the graduate level and in research these same concepts are studied in a Walrasian framework, and the tools are a variety of mathematical techniques including higher-level calculus such as optimal control theory, game theory, set theory, and topology.[1]

In macroeconomics, undergraduate and graduate education differ; on the undergraduate level students learn modified neo-Keynesian macro modeling in which interest rates, price levels, and income levels are determined in a multi-market model. The tools are generally geometric (IS/LM-AS/AD), algebraic (matrix algebra), and simple analysis or calculus. The central concept taught is the nature of multi-market interactions with some understanding of the workings of monetary and fiscal policy. Much more real-world terminology and institutional information are taught than are taught in micro. On the graduate and research levels there is less consistency in what is taught; in most graduate schools and in research, mainstream macro is closely related to micro, but how it is related differs significantly among schools. While the central concepts are the same among schools, their interpretation and the tools used to present them are substantially different.

The third set of concepts making up mainstream economics is classical statistical analysis. On the undergraduate level the concentration is on significance testing and regression analysis (correlations). On the graduate level the same concepts are taught, although the level is higher. Research normally involves the use of high-level econometric techniques.

Combined, micro, macro, and econometrics make up the core of mainstream economic theory. As students learn this core and as economists work with these concepts, they learn both economic and business terminology and acquire institutional knowledge either by explicit teaching or by osmosis. This terminology and institutional knowledge, while not part of the central concepts, might be considered a fourth part of mainstream economics.

**There Is Much Good
in Mainstream Economics**

Each of the three central areas of mainstream economics can be criticized for both its content and its tools. I, for one, believe that the content of all three core subjects is worth knowing. For example, classical statistical analysis provides students with tools they can use to analyze and understand otherwise confusing data. Correlation, significance, and probability have meaning and are useful concepts. Similarly, in microeconomics, concepts such as opportunity costs and marginal decision making provide students with useful tools for all types of decision-making problems; I am continually amazed at how few students who have not taken microeconomics understand marginal decision analysis. The deep microeconomic insights about efficiency are far less convincing to me, but to go into why would take at least a book. But even without much faith in these insights, I can defend microeconomics since much of it is not tied to those insights. In fact, most students and many economists never get at those issues.

In macroeconomics there is also much that is good. One learns how to structure a multi-market model and the terminology used by most people to discuss macroeconomic policy. Some relationship between money, deficits, prices, and interest rates exists in the world, and these relationships need to be taught. Unfortunately, we don't understand much about these relationships, but teaching the general process of modeling simultaneously with macroeconomic terminology makes sense; it allows students to see one method of interrelating these variables. Quite clearly there are many other ways for these variables to interrelate, but you must begin somewhere.

The success of mainstream economics is apparent in what economists do who do not remain economists; they move into business management positions and a wide variety of executive positions. Unemployed English and history teachers become cab drivers; unemployed economists become successful executives, businessmen, or entrepreneurs. The reason economists succeed in other areas is not due to the institutional knowledge they have gained from studying economics but to the approach to decision making that it teaches. Individuals trained in mainstream economics can reason and think effectively; they can often make hard decisions and see interrelations that individuals with other training cannot. Learning mainstream economic analysis teaches students to think with an almost sickening reasonableness.[2]

In summary, mainstream economics provides a general framework for understanding the events that shape our lives. It is not the only framework, but it is a reasonably good one, especially if students are simultaneously taught methodological pluralism: There are other reasonable ways to organize one's thinking, which for certain issues are highly illuminating.

What's Wrong with Mainstream Economics?

If I believe there is so much good in mainstream economics, why am I a critic? The reason is that mainstream economics takes a good thing and overdoes it and in doing so leaves out other good things that could make mainstream economics much better. It has become so obsessed with a particular formalistic framework that it oftentimes misses rather obvious insights about the functioning of the economy.

The normal argument in favor of formalism is well known—that formalism is necessary to maintain logical structure and clarity of thought. To some degree this argument is true. Important insights have come from formal models, and I, as an informal mainstream economist, am a major consumer of those insights. Were good economists not working on such formal models, I would likely change my research interests and work on these formal questions. But I believe that mainstream economics has far exceeded that level.

In mainstream economics the tools, specifically formal modeling and using sophisticated econometric techniques, too often become ends; playing with the tools becomes a game. I am not arguing against games; games are useful in sharpening economists' analytical minds and thus have an important role to play in economics. But in mainstream economics the game has become almost an end in itself, so that many mainstream economists lose sight of how to apply to reality the lessons learned from the game. As that connection is lost, the tools become even more esoteric.

In physics, there is the law of significant digits, which states that all calculations should be carried out to the same level of exactness. My objection to the formalism of mainstream economics is that it violates that law. Certain aspects of mainstream economics are carried out to twenty digits, while other aspects are rounded off at two.

To be clear about my objection, I should state that my problem is not that some members of the mainstream work on formalistic models of esoteric issues; my complaint is that to a large degree the normal mainstream ''good economist,'' as well as the superstars, work only on such issues. At some point the high-tech game playing must be complemented with other useful activities and concepts such as the mundane skills and tools of handling data, collecting institutional knowledge, and informally integrating large amounts of data in noncompatible forms. Currently, if a problem can't be set up as a complicated model or if data cannot be transposed into a consistent time series and analyzed with sophisticated econometric techniques, they won't be considered by mainstream economics. How does one handle nonquantifiable or nongeneralizable data? How does one recognize when and how sociological aspects influence economic decisions? These are important skills, but because they cannot be translated into a neat model (or, if they can, the model is too simple to capture all but the most obvious influences), these skills are not taught or valued by the profession.

Mundane skills and institutional sensibilities should complement the high-tech analytic skills of mainstream economics. But they do not, and hence economics has lost its ability to relate to reality. For example, marginal analysis is a good first step in analyzing production and pricing problems of firms, but it is only a first step. Most production decisions are lumpy multi-dimensional decisions where objective functions and arguments cannot be neatly specified in continuous maximization problems. Most mainstream economists never make the jump.

The same argument can be made about IS/LM analysis. Macro IS/LM models provide one method through which the real and nominal sectors can interact, but if accepted too literally they lead economists to miss other ways in which the two can interact.

In summary, what is wrong with mainstream economics is not so much what is taught but what is not; it is not so much the methods researchers use but the methods they don't use. Specifically, mainstream economics does not teach sufficient self-criticalness; it does not teach that there are many acceptable ways to approach a problem and that mainstream is not the only way.[3] But all these are things that could be added to the mainstream; they do not need to replace it.

Value Judgments and Mainstream Economics

Critics level many charges other than those presented above. Probably the charge heard most often—from Marxist, Post-Keynesian, and Institutionalist critics—is that mainstream economics is value-laden, that it idealizes and gives students and practitioners a bias in favor of the market.

These charges are misplaced. In saying that these charges are misplaced, I make no claim that neo-classical economics is value-free. Values are inherent in questions it doesn't pose and in its formalism, but these inherent values seem no worse, and indeed somewhat less value-laden, than are the approaches of the nonmainstream groups. To call an approach value-laden, a critic must go beyond that obvious criticism and argue that mainstream economics is more value-laden than other approaches. This is not the case; mainstream economists hold a wide range of positions on the market and on the role of the state. Using the rational individual decision approach, one can arrive at significant criticisms of the market and can accept the need for sociological and institutional limitations on individual decisions. There is no one set of policies that follows from mainstream economics.

The same cannot be said for the critics who challenge the content of mainstream economics. Marxists, Austrians, Post-Keynesians, and Institutionalists have inherent values that show up much more clearly than do the values in mainstream economics. One sees few conservative Marxists, Post-Keynesians, or Institutionalists, and no liberal (as opposed to libertarian) Austrians.

Moreover, nonmainstream groups both feverishly protect their turf and seem unwilling to allow any dissent within their ranks. I have seen Austrian economists booed out at Post-Keynesian meetings, Institutionalists ridiculed by Austrians, and all other approaches classified as useless by Marxists. Personally I have received vituperative rejections from Institutionalist and Post-Keynesian journals for submitting papers that did not toe the party line. When I was a graduate student attending a student-run seminar on Marxist theory and asked whether class could be interpreted within a monopoly type of model, I was told that even to think in such terms meant that I did not belong there. Such incidents are personal, but I have found no evidence that non-mainstream groups are any less value-laden than is mainstream economics. In any case, I have come to the conclusion that mainstream economics, while certainly not value-free, is more nearly so than the alternatives.[4]

Is Mainstream Economics' Overemphasis on Tools Cause for Its Overthrow?

Above, I argued that a central problem of mainstream economics is that much of its content has been lost in overformal tools and that tools have replaced content. Such criticisms are insufficient to condemn mainstream economics, for two reasons. First, the overformality is a result of forces that are inherent in the institutional structure in the United States, and any approach that becomes mainstream will face those same forces. Thus this criticism must be tempered by a sense of reality. Second, there are strong arguments for formality which go beyond those stated above—that formality is helpful in teaching logical thought processes.

These other arguments, which make me hesitant to criticize the foundation of mainstream economics, have been less often articulated. The first was pointed out to me by Axel Leijonhufvud. Commenting on the writing of the economic critic G.L.S. Schackle, Leijonhufvud said that Schackle's writings were wonderful but he hoped that none of his students would discover them because those who did would start thinking about too many issues, too soon, and generally become hopelessly confused. An analogy can be made to sex: Sex is wonderful, but it is good to keep children away from its pleasures until they have the maturity to handle it. It may be wise to keep students in the dark about nonformal approaches to problems so that their analytic faculties can have time to develop working on issues that can be handled. Good nonformal analysis is beautiful, but it is much more difficult to do than is good formal analysis. The existence of formal analysis and good training in formal analysis keep nonformal analysis within acceptable bounds; without it, informal analysis would often sink into hopeless verbiage.

A related argument in favor of formalism holds even if one believes that formal models do no good in helping economists understand the economy. Formal models are useful in weeding out those who have analytic ability from those who do not. Modeling ability serves as a signaling device or a hurdle over which future economists must jump. Knowing that they have jumped these hurdles makes one more likely to take their nonformal analysis seriously. What is studied is less important than the fact that something which exercises one's logical faculties is studied. Thus much of mainstream economics can be justified in the same way that we justify the study of English literature and ancient Greek philosophy.

Even if one is unconvinced (as I am) by the above arguments for formalism, it can be accepted as inevitable; formalism is inherent in the institutional structure of the U.S. educational system. In the economics profession most of the leaders are in academia. To succeed as an academic one must teach reasonably interesting courses that students think are good, and one must publish. Both those ends push toward formalism.

In teaching, one quickly discovers that teaching models is much easier than teaching good nonformal analysis. Models have solutions that are either right or wrong. Moreover, students like models because they provide certainty, and subjective elements don't enter in. As that happens, the nature of the classes changes; classes get larger, making nonformal analysis almost impossible to teach. Nonformal analysis cannot be taught in a multiple-choice exam environment.

The second element of success in an academic environment is publishing. Working on formal models that don't relate to reality provides a higher payoff than working on articles based on in-depth institutional knowledge. If one learns a technique, one can apply it to different areas and hence get five or ten articles out of it. If one learns a specific area, one can get, at most, two articles out of it and those most likely in specialized rather than general interest journals.

The same set of incentives toward formalism exists with statistics. Applying high-level techniques is more likely to lead to multiple articles than is applying low-level techniques with large amounts of institutional data. Moreover, there is little incentive to be honest about how little our statistical studies are telling us. All mainstream economists know that models are not developed independently of the data and that most classical statistical tests do not apply, yet we go on running such tests and mining data because doing so leads to publication and consulting jobs. Those incentives will be there regardless of what is the mainstream of the profession, so we cannot use mainstream's formalism as a reason to overthrow it.[5]

Mainstream Economics Is Institutionally Successful

For all its faults, and perhaps because of them, mainstream economics has been successful. It gets jobs for economists—the critics as well as the mainstream economists. For those who want to change economics, I suggest looking to other fields. Law and legal theory are a mess; sociology, political science, and anthropology are all in much greater disarray than is economics.

The United States has somewhere around 150,000 economists. Most college students take at least one course in economics in their career. Economists are talked about by the press as making up a legitimate profession, and they have a large number of publishing outlets. Mainstream economics must be doing something right.

Even the promarket bias of mainstream economics may work in critics' favor. Just as formalism allows nonformalists to operate, mainstream's promarket bias may allow critics more chance to express themselves than they would otherwise have. The existence of economists in a society is not preordained, and mainstream's success in the classroom and in interacting with business and government has provided critics with more, not less, opportunity to make their arguments.

To the Austrian critics I address the following challenge. Think of it from an Austrian perspective: What has developed has developed for reasons, some of which we can and some of which we cannot understand. In replacing mainstream economics with something else, we are liable to do more harm than good.

What Do Critics Have to Offer?

My defense of mainstream economics has been defensive; clearly I don't believe mainstream economics is the only way or even necessarily the best way to study economic reality. But I defend it because, compared to the alternatives, there is no comparison. Critics have simply not established even an outline of a viable alternative. In fact, most critics spend much of their time talking about methodology, leaving them little time to contribute to public knowledge about the economy. Let's assume for the moment that one dissident group took control of the profession. What would change? I just don't know. Thus, for me, at this point in time, mainstream economics is the only game in town.

Notes

1. The frameworks and tools differ substantially among graduate schools.

2. Among noneconomists, reasonableness is not rated so highly. In explaining why she felt our relationship had problems, a former girlfriend (an English teacher) told me that the problem was that I was so . . . so . . . reasonable.

3. I am not arguing that other models should necessarily be taught or that other methods should be emphasized. But even if mainstream economics doesn't teach these other methods, it could survey them and make its researchers aware of, and perhaps more willing to consider, those other ways of approaching problems.

4. Some of the defensiveness of dissident groups can be explained by a "circling the wagons" mentality, but heaven help us if that mentality should become the mainstream.

5. In statistics, there has been some pressure to change, but that pressure has come from within mainstream economics, not from the dissident groups outside the mainstream. The fact that there can be some pressure for change from within speaks well for mainstream economics.

Works Cited and Related References

Barro, Robert. 1984. *Macroeconomics*. New York: Wiley.

Barro, Robert, and H. Grossman. 1976. *Money, Employment and Inflation*. New York: Cambridge University Press.

Becker, Howard, et al. 1961. *Boys in White: Student Culture in Medical School*. Chicago: University of Chicago Press.

———. 1970. *Sociological Work: Method and Substance*. Chicago: Aldine.

Clower, Robert W. 1989. "The State of Economics: Hopeless But Not Serious?" In *The Spread of Economic Ideas*, ed. David Colander and A.W. Coats. New York: Cambridge University Press.

Coats. A.W. (Bob). 1985. "The Sociology of Science: Its Application to Economics." Duke University, mimeo.

Colander, David. 1979. "Rationality, Expectation and Functional Finance." In *Essays in Post Keynesian Inflation*, ed. James Gapinski and Charles Rockwood. Cambridge, MA: Ballinger Publishing Co.

———. 1982. "Stagflation and Competition." *Journal of Post Keynesian Economics* (Fall).

———. 1985. "Why an Incomes Policy Makes an Economy More Efficient." In *Macroeconomic Conflicts and Social Institutions*, ed. S. Maital. Boston: Ballinger Press.

———. 1986. *Macroeconomics*. Glenview, IL: Scott, Foresman.

———. 1988. "The Evolution of Keynesian Economics: From Keynesian to New Classical to New Keynesian." In *Keynes and Public Policy after Fifty Years*, ed. Omar Hamouda and John Smithen. Aldershot, England: Edward Elgar.

———. 1989. "The Invisible Hand of Truth." In *The Spread of Economic Ideas*, ed. David Colander and A.W. Coats. New York: Cambridge University Press.

Colander, David, and A.W. Coats, eds. 1989. *The Spread of Economic Ideas*. New York: Cambridge Universty Press.

Colander, David, and Robert Guthrie. 1980–81. "Great Expectations: What the Dickens Do Rational Expectations Mean?" *Journal of Post Keynesian Economics* 3 no. 2 (Winter).

Colander, David, and Arjo Klamer. 1987. "The Making of an Economist." *Journal of Economic Perspectives* 1 (Fall).

Colander, David, and Mancur Olson. 1984. "Coalitions and Macroeconomics." In *Neoclassical Political Economy*, ed. David Colander. Boston: Ballinger Press.

Davis, Paul, and Gustav Papanek. 1984. "Faculty Ratings of Major Economics Departments by Citations." *American Economic Review* (March).

Dewald, William, et al. 1986. "Replication in Empirical Economics." *American Economic Review* (September).

Frey, Bruno, et al. 1984. "Consensus and Dissension Among Economists: An Empirical Inquiry." *American Economic Review* (March).

Friedman, Milton. 1977. *Friedman and Galbraith*. Vancouver, Canada: The Fraser Institute.

Galbraith, John Kenneth. 1936. "Monopoly Power and Price Rigidities." *Quarterly Journal of Economics* (May).

————. 1941. "The Selection and Timing of Inflation Controls." *The Review of Economics and Statistics* (May).

————. 1946. "Reflections on Price Control." *Quarterly Journal of Economics* (August).

————. 1947. "The Disequilibrium System." *American Economic Review* (June).

————. 1952a. *American Capitalism: The Concept of Countervailing Power.* Cambridge, MA: Riverside Press.

————. 1952b. *A Theory of Price Control.* Cambridge, MA: Harvard University Press. Reissued, 1980, as *A Theory of Price Control: The Classic Account.*

————. 1957. "Market Structure and Stabilization Policy." *Review of Economics and Statistics* (May).

————. 1967. "Galbraith on Galbraith." *The New York Times Book Review* (June 25).

————. 1977. *The Galbraith Reader.* Ipswich, MA: Gambit.

————. 1980. *A Theory of Price Control: The Classic Account.* Cambridge, MA: Harvard University Press.

————. 1981. *A Life In Our Times.* Boston: Houghton Mifflin.

Galbraith, John Kenneth, and Henry Dennison. 1938. *Modern Competition and Business Policy.* New York: Oxford University Press.

Gourman, Jack. 1983. *Rating of Graduate and Professional Programs in American and International Universities.* Washington, DC: National Education Standard.

Graves, Philip, et al. 1982. "Economics Departmental Rankings: Research Incentives, Constraints, and Efficiency." *American Economic Review* (December).

Grubel, Herbert, and Lawrence Boland. 1986. "On the Efficient Use of Mathematics in Economics: Some Theory, Facts and Results of an Opinion Survey." *Kyklos*, fasc. 3.

Hession, Charles. 1972. *Kenneth Galbraith and His Critics.* New York: Mentor.

Keynes, John Maynard. 1936. *The General Theory of Employment, Inflation, and Money.* New York: Harcourt.

Klamer, Arjo. 1983. *Conversations with Economists: New Classical Economists and Opponents Speak Out on the Current Controversy in Macroeconomics.* Totowa, NJ: Rowman and Allanheld.

Klamer, Arjo, and David Colander. 1990. *The Making of an Economist.* Boulder, CO: Westview Press, 1990.

Kuttner, Robert. 1985. "The Poverty of Economics." *Atlantic Monthly* (February).

Landreth, Harry, and David Colander. 1989. *History of Economic Theory,* 2d ed. Boston: Houghton Mifflin.

Leamer, Edward. 1983. "Let's Take the Con Out of Econometrics." *American Economic Review* (March).

———. 1988. "Things That Bother Me." *The Economic Record* (December).

Leijonhufvud, Axel. 1968. *Keynesian Economics and the Economics of Keynes.* London: Oxford University Press.

Malinvaud, E. 1977. *The Theory of Unemployment Reconsidered.* New York: Wiley.

McCain, Katherine W. 1984. "The Author Cocitation Structure of Macroeconomics." *Scientometrics,* no. 5.

McCloskey, Donald. 1983. "The Rhetoric of Economics." *Journal of Economic Literature* (June).

National Academy of Sciences. 1982. "An Assessment of Research-Doctorate Programs in the United States Social and Behavioral Sciences."

Navasky, V.S. 1967. "Galbraith on Galbraith." *The New York Times Book Review* (June 15).

Owen, Wyn, and Larry Cross. 1984. *Guide to Graduate Study in Economics, Agricultural Economics, and Doctoral Degrees in Business Administration.* Boulder, CO: Economic Institute.

Phelps, Edmund. 1970. *Microeconomic Foundations of Employment and Inflation Theory.* New York: Norton, 1970.

Plum, Terry. 1987. "On Quantifying Economic Ideas." *Journal of Economic and Monetary Affairs* (July).

Robinson, Joan. 1952. Review of *American Capitalism,* by John Kenneth Galbraith. *Economic Journal* (December).

Samuelson, Paul. 1964. "The *General Theory* in 1936." In *Keynes's General Theory,* ed. R. Lekachman. New York: St. Martin's Press.

———. 1948. *Economics* (1st edition). New York: McGraw-Hill.

Samuelson, Robert. 1988. *Newsweek* (August 31).

Sen, Amartya. 1970. "The Impossibility of a Paretian Liberal." *Journal of Political Economy* 78 (Jan.–Feb.).

Solow, Robert M. 1989. "Faith, Hope, and Clarity." In *The Spread of Economic Ideas,* ed. David Colander and A.W. Coats. New York: Cambridge University Press.

Spellman, William, and Bruce Gabriel. 1978. "Graduate Students in Economics: 1970–74." *American Economic Review* (March).

Stigler, George. [1975] 1982. *The Economist as Preacher*. Chicago: University of Chicago Press.

Tarshis, Lorie. 1947. *The Elements of Economics, an Introduction to the Theory of Price and Employment*. Boston: Houghton Mifflin.

Taylor, John, and Robert Hall. 1986. *Macroeconomics*. New York: Norton.

Ward, Benjamin. 1972. *What's Wrong with Economics*. New York: Basic Books.

Weintraub, Roy. 1983. "On the Existence of a Competitive Equilibrium: 1930–1954." *Journal of Economic Literature* (March).

———. 1986. *General Equilibrium Analysis*. Cambridge: Cambridge University Press.

Whitley, Richard. 1984. *The Intellectual and Social Organization of the Sciences*. London: Oxford University Press.

Index

About the Author

David Colander, Christian A. Johnson Distinguished Professor of Economics at Middlebury College, has authored, coauthored, or edited thirteen books and over fifty articles, including *MAP, A Market Anti-Inflation Plan,* with Abba Lerner, and *The Making of an Economist,* with Arjo Klamer. One of the youngest economists to receive a distinguished professorship, Colander earned his M.Phil. and Ph.D. at Columbia University, a B.A. at Columbia College, and studied at the University of Birmingham in England and the Wilhelmsburg Gymnasium in Germany. He is on the board of directors of the Eastern Economics Association and a member of the board of advisors for the *Journal of Economic Perspectives.*